how2become

Achieve 100% Series
Pass Your A-Levels
With A*s

www.How2Become.com

As part of this product you have also received FREE access to online tests that will help you to pass your A-Levels.

To gain access, simply go to:

www.MyEducationalTests.co.uk

Get more products for passing any test at:

www.How2Become.com

Orders: Please contact How2Become Ltd, Suite 14, 50 Churchill Square Business Centre, Kings Hill, Kent ME19 4YU.

You can order through Amazon.co.uk under ISBN: 9781911259152, via the website www. How2Become.com or through Gardners.com.

ISBN: 9781911259152

First published in 2017 by How2Become Ltd.

Typeset by How2Become Ltd.

Disclaimer

Every effort has been made to ensure that the information contained within this guide is accurate at the time of publication. How2Become Ltd is not responsible for anyone failing any part of any selection process as a result of the information contained within this guide. How2Become Ltd and their authors cannot accept any responsibility for any errors or omissions within this guide, however caused. No responsibility for loss or damage occasioned by any person acting, or refraining from action, as a result of the material in this publication can be accepted by How2Become Ltd.

The information within this guide does not represent the views of any third party service or organisation.

Contents

Introduction

Welcome to *Pass Your A-Levels With A*s*. In this guide, we'll be covering everything you need to know in order to ace your A-Levels. From coursework to exams, revision to planning, you'll learn tips from the experts, and people who have taken and succeeded in their A-Levels over the past few years.

What are A-Levels?

A-Levels are advanced courses that students usually take between the ages of 16 and 18, during years 11 and 12. This means that A-Levels come after GCSEs, and students generally need to get good GCSE grades before they can start an A-Level course. 'A-Level' is short for 'General Certificate of Education Advanced Level.' It's awarded to students who pass the coursework and exams that make up an A-Level course.

How are they Different to GCSEs?

The first (and biggest) difference between A-Levels and GCSEs is that A-Levels take things up a gear in terms of difficulty. Just as GCSE is a step up from KS3, A-Level is much more demanding than GCSE. No matter what subjects you take, you'll need to learn new ideas and techniques, retain more information, learn how to answer new types of questions, and approach things in new ways. In many subjects, the focus of assessment will change too. For example, History at GCSE level focuses more on your ability to recall important events and facts. In contrast, A-Level History requires you to critically analyse events, structure arguments and examine cause and effect – as well as recall important information. Other subjects also differ from their GCSE counterparts in similar ways.

A-Level courses are offered in a wide range of subjects, and there is far more on offer than at GCSE. Also, unlike GCSE level, there are no mandatory courses that you must take. So, if you hated Maths at GCSE, you can drop it when you get to A-Level. This means that you get more freedom with your choices. This, combined with a wealth of subjects to choose from, will guarantee that you are spoilt for choice!

Students at A-Level tend to take around 3 or 4 subjects, and these are often based on what they enjoyed or did well at during their GCSEs. However, there are some entirely new subjects that you won't have been taught before. This means that you need to think very carefully about what subjects you want to take, before jumping into them.

Here is a full list of all subjects offered at A-Level. Bear in mind that not all of these will be offered at your school, so check with your teachers about what subjects are available to you.

Accounting	**Afrikaans**	Ancient History
Anthropology	**Arabic**	Archaeology
Architecture	Art and Design	**Bengali**
Biblical Hebrew	Biology	Business Studies
Chemistry	**Chinese**	Classics
Computing	Computer Science	Creative Writing
Critical Thinking	Dance	Design and Technology
Divinity (Theology)	Drama and Theatre Studies	**Dutch**
Economics	Electronics	Engineering
English Language	English Literature	Film Studies
Food Studies	**French**	Further Mathematics
Geography	Geology	**German**
Government and Politics	Graphic Design	**Greek (Modern)**
Gujarati	Health and Social Care	**Hebrew (Modern)**

Hindi	Hinduism	History
History of Art	Human Biology	Humanities
ICT	**Irish**	Islamic Studies
Italian	**Japanese**	**Latin**
Law	Leisure Studies	Leisure and Tourism
Mathematics	Media Studies	Music
Music Technology	**Punjabi**	Performing Arts
Persian	Philosophy	Physical Education
Physics	**Polish**	**Portuguese**
Psychology	Religious Studies	Research Projects
Russian	Sociology	**Spanish**
Statistics	**Tamil**	**Telugu**
Turkish	**Urdu**	**Welsh**

(Please note - all subjects written in **bold** are languages)

A-Levels differ from GCSEs in a few other ways too. Firstly, A-Levels are not linear in the same way that GCSEs are. At GCSE level, you start a course at the beginning of year 10, and take your exams in the Spring term of year 11. So, there's almost a two-year gap between starting your GCSEs and taking any exams in them.

A-Level is quite different, because it's split into two different certificates – AS and A2. AS is taken during the first year of your A-Levels, which tends to be year 12. AS level is generally easier than A2, which is taken in the second year of A-Level: year 13. Students who take four subjects for their first year of A-Level tend to only take three to A2 level. In this case, students will end up with 3 full A-Levels as well as one AS level. Universities and employers alike find this completely acceptable, so don't feel forced to take all four subjects to A2 level. However, if you find yourself drawn to all four of your AS subjects, and want to complete them all at A2, feel free to do so!

Depending on how many A-Levels you take, your results could look like any of the following:

	5 A-Levels	**4 A-Levels**	**3 A-Levels**
Take all to A2 level	5 A-Levels 0 AS levels	4 A-Levels 0 AS levels	3 A-Levels 0 AS levels
Drop one subject at AS level	4 A-Levels 1 AS level	3 A-Levels 1 AS level	2 A-Levels 1 AS level

Another difference between A-Level and GCSE is that A-Levels are graded in letters, as opposed to GCSEs which are graded in numbers. This could change in the future, but as of 2017 the A-Level grades are as follows:

A*	A	B	C	D	E	U

As you can imagine, 'A*' is the highest grade available at A-Level, whilst the lowest grade is 'U'. The minimum grade required to pass at A-Level is 'E'. However, just because this is the pass grade, it doesn't mean you should aim for the bare minimum of 'E'! If you're looking to go into higher education such as a university degree, you're probably going to need a much better grade than this.

Why do they Matter?

While A-Levels are very different to GCSEs in a lot of ways, they are fundamentally similar, because they both shape the direction of your career, and possibly your life as well. 'Failing' your A-Levels won't ruin your life, but better results will certainly open more opportunities to you. As previously mentioned, you'll need much higher than an 'E' grade in order to get into university, and many employers will be looking for higher A-Level grades as well. Simply put, A-Levels matter because they determine where you're going to go next. The best universities in the UK tend to have minimum entry requirements of 'A's and 'A*'s, usually in at least three A-Level subjects. Others will usually accept nothing lower than 'C's. So, you want to make sure that you do well at A-Level.

Moreover, studying for A-Levels will assist you in gaining the skills required at university. For example, if you want to study History at degree level, you're going to need to do the following:

- Read and cite sources to support your argument;

- Write long-form essays which critically assess events and people rather than just describing them;

- Learn key terminology as well as historical theories and interpretations.

This isn't everything that you'd need to know, but these are three of the key areas a History student would need to focus on at degree level in order to get a strong grade. While you won't do all of these things in great detail at A-Level, you will be introduced to these ideas. For example, History coursework taken at A-Level usually requires students to use primary and secondary sources to strengthen their argument. At degree level, this is vital for almost any essay-based subject (such as English Literature, Philosophy, Theology, Classics, and Anthropology) – not just History.

Likewise, A-Level is a step-up from GCSE in many subjects, because it encourages and demands critical analysis, not just description of events. This is also very important for students at degree level. University examiners usually expect you to construct some form of critical argument based on the topic and information given, rather than just regurgitate facts. A-Level acts as a bridge between GCSE and degree level here, because it will teach you to think critically about the material that you're reading. So, if you're planning on going into higher education, studying hard for your A-Levels benefits you in two different ways:

1. A-Levels are the qualifications required to get into higher education such as university.

2. Studying A-Levels will give you the knowledge and skills necessary in order to perform well at degree level.

But what if you don't want to go to university? Perhaps you have your eyes set on a certain profession that doesn't necessarily require such high results at A-Level. In this case, A-Levels serve as a great place to gain knowledge and explore areas that you find fascinating. The benefit of A-Levels is that you get to pick which ones you take, so you can make sure that you find something that piques your interest. Whatever you plan to do, it doesn't hurt to give A-Levels your best shot, especially if you find something enjoyable about them.

Achieving an A*

You might have noticed that this book is called *Pass Your A-Levels With A*s*. The aim is to unlock your full potential at A-Level, and give you all of the necessary tips and techniques to get top marks. However, if you want to aim for an 'A*', you'll need to know about its specific requirements.

Until 2010, there was no such thing as an 'A*' at A-Level. Even if you obtained full marks in every exam that you sat, and every piece of coursework you completed, you would only get a maximum of an 'A'. At the time this was no problem, since universities and employers were aware of this situation, and wouldn't penalise students for not having 'A*s'.

As of 2010, the situation regarding 'A*s' at A-Levels has changed, and they're now obtainable. However, the conditions for obtaining an 'A*' are slightly unusual, and not as straightforward as getting a certain percentage overall, like all of the other grades.

Most of the grades at A-Level take an average of all your scores, each with its own weighting. For example, if you get an 'A' in one exam (worth 50%), and a 'C' in another exam (also worth 50%), you'll likely get somewhere around a 'B' grade. This means that, the better you perform in one exam, the more marks you'll have banked, and the better your position is for other exams. If you were aiming for a 'B', and got an 'A' in your first exam, you could be quite comfortable getting a 'C' and scoring a 'B' overall.

However, getting an 'A*' is different. To achieve this grade, you need the following:

- An overall 'A' grade (80%) across your entire A-Level;

- At least 90% in each of your A2 level modules.

The difference here is that you specifically need to be scoring 90% in your A2 modules, in order to get an 'A*' overall. In other words, you need to get the following in order to get an 'A*' overall:

- An average of 80% at AS level;

• 90% across all modules at A2 level.

So, you need to go above and beyond in order to score an 'A*' at A-Level. The 90% grade boundary specifically at A2 level means that you can't rely on 'banked' marks from AS level. So, a lot is riding on getting a high score at A2 level.

Finally, 'A*s' can't be obtained at AS level. If you want to get an 'A*' overall, you just need to focus on getting a minimum of 80% at AS level, followed by 90% at A2.

Who is this Book For?

If you're reading this book, you're probably aiming high in terms of academic achievement. Perhaps you're looking for strategies to use in a particular subject, or perhaps you want more general advice on how to study and how to perform well in exams and coursework. In this book, you will be introduced to general and specific revision techniques which will allow you to unlock your full potential.

Alternatively, you may be completely new to A-Levels, and looking for a head-start to put you in the right direction. This book will help you identify what kind of learner you are, and then give advice on how to make the most out of different learning styles. For instance, you might be a visual learner, in which case you may wish to use videos and mind maps to commit information to memory in a visual way.

It may be the case that you are part-way through your A-Levels and are feeling stressed or nervous about what comes next. This book will give you some techniques and strategies for handling stress, as well as reassuring you that good results can still be salvaged, no matter what point you're at in your studies.

If you're reading this book, you're already demonstrating that you want to go further than the classroom when it comes to A-Levels. This is great. It shows that you have a strong work ethic, and puts you in an excellent position when it comes to the harder elements of the course.

Finally, you might be a parent reading this on behalf of your child, or perhaps you are reading it in anticipation of your child's future A-Levels. We will include 'advice for parents' sections where applicable. These will highlight ways in which you can help prepare your child for their A-Levels.

The aim of this book is to provide advice no matter what your situation. If you're reading this because you are sitting A-Levels yourself, or you're reading this on behalf of a family member sitting their A-Levels, then this book will apply to you. Everyone will sit exams, and so the next two chapters are certainly applicable to your situation. Equally, some students will have to do coursework, and so a chapter is devoted to that as well. The final chapter will focus on a selection of subjects, giving subject-specific information on each.

If you've completed your GCSEs, you'll be familiar with a number of techniques that can help you on your way to success. Regardless, make sure to read the following chapters, since there may be tips and tricks that you might not already know!

General Study Techniques

In this chapter, we'll be considering how to get started with your A-Level studies. Before getting into your revision, making a timetable or doing practice questions, it's important to figure out a few things first. In particular, you want to know what revision methods work for you. This is important because finding the most effective revision strategies that suit you, will make studying much easier and much more efficient. Working hard is very important, but it's also important to work smart. By this, we mean that you should focus your efforts on revision techniques that make the best use of your time.

In this chapter, we'll be focusing on the following:

- Why revision is important;

- The 3 different kinds of learning: visual, aural and kinaesthetic;

- Revision strategies for each learning style.

Why Should I Revise?

Just like at GCSE, A-Levels require lots of knowledge in order for students to perform well. You'll be tested on a number of things during A-Level, but knowledge is the foundation for all of it. After all, you can't answer the questions in a Maths paper if you don't know your logarithms, indices laws, quadratic equations and methods of integration. Likewise, you can't critically analyse a novel in an exam if you don't know its themes, and don't have some quotes ready in your head to support your argument. No matter which way you look at A-Levels, revision is going to play a key part in success.

Revision is the most influential factor in success at most academic levels, including A-Level. You might feel that you are naturally intelligent and don't need to revise, or maybe you've been very successful at GCSE and think you can coast through A-Level. Sadly, this isn't the case – you will need to put hard work into your A-Levels in order to get a satisfactory result.

As mentioned previously, A-Levels are the second rung on the qualifications ladder. They're the gateway to higher education, as well as a significant boost to your employability. Therefore, it's vital that you get off to a good start. Moreover, learning smart revision techniques will equip you well for higher education and the working world, so it pays to put in the hours at A-Level and figure out what works best for you.

The Three Types of Learning

There are three major ways that people revise and absorb information. These are:

* **Visual** – This involves using visual aids such as note-taking and creative mapping of information, to commit things to memory.

* **Aural** – The use of videos, music or other recordings to allow information to sink in.

* **Kinaesthetic** – Using activities which involve interaction, to remember key details (such as flashcards and revision games).

Different paths will work better for different people, but also bear in mind that certain subjects will also suit these methods differently. For example, Maths may be better suited to visual learning than aural learning, because mathematics (sums and equations) is more visually-oriented than other subjects. However, certain rules or formulae could be learned by placing notes around your study space, if you're a kinaesthetic learner.

Essentially, you will need to experiment with different styles in order to find which ones best suit you, but you will also need to discover which works for each of your subjects. In the next three sections, we will examine the different methods of learning in more detail. Additionally, each method will be paired with the subjects which best suit it, as well as how to identify which style matches your own.

The quickest way to figure out what kind of learner you are, is to think of what works best for you when trying to remember something. When someone needs to explain to you how to do something, what sinks in the best? Do you learn by watching others doing it first, or by listening to their explanation? Alternatively, you might learn best by giving it a try yourself. Use the following quick guide to figure out what kind of learner you might be:

- **Visual** – You learn best by watching others or reading information. If you're learning a technique in a game, sport, or other activity, you would prefer to watch videos of others doing it, watching people do it in real-life, or by reading explanations. You might also learn from looking at images or diagrams.

- **Aural** – Listening is your preferred style of learning. You would rather ask for and listen to directions rather than look at a map. If you were learning something new, you'd rather listen to an explanation and follow the instructions.

- **Kinaesthetic** – You learn by doing things rather than just listening or reading. Rather than being told how to do something, you try to do it yourself. You prefer practical, energetic ways of learning as opposed to the traditional methods of reading, listening and note-taking.

Learning Style Quiz

The following learning style quiz can be used to figure out which of the above learning styles suits you best. Once you're done, head to the answers section, where all will be revealed!

1. If you were watching an advertisement for a product on TV, how would you most likely react?

A) You'd notice the imagery, colours and other things happening on screen.

B) You'd recognise and listen to the music, and maybe even hum along if you knew it well enough.

C) You'd remember a time when you saw or interacted with the product in real life.

2. You're using a programme on your computer and can't figure out how to perform a specific task. How would you learn how to do it?

A) Watch an online video tutorial of someone doing it.

B) Ask someone to tell you how to do it.

C) Attempt it yourself until you figure out how it's done.

---

3. If you had to learn lines for a theatre production, how would you do it?

A) Sit down with the script and read your lines in your head.

B) Read the lines out loud to yourself.

C) Get together with a few other people and act out your scene(s).

---

4. You need to remember someone's postcode, so that you can find their house. How do you best remember it?

A) Visualise the letters and numbers.

B) Repeat the postcode out loud to yourself.

C) Write it down.

---

5. You're doing some fairly simple mental arithmetic. How would you solve the sum?

A) By visualising it in your head.

B) By saying the numbers and the operation out loud, step by step.

C) By counting or subtracting on your fingers, or by using objects nearby (such as counting pens and pencils).

6. Which of the following would you most likely do for fun?

A) Watch TV.

B) Listen to a radio show or podcast.

C) Play a video game.

7. You're queueing for a theme park ride and the wait time is quite long. Which of the following would you most notice whilst in the queue?

A) The decorations in the queueing areas.

B) The music or sound effects playing in the background.

C) How long it's been since you last moved in the queue.

8. If you saw the word "apple" written down, how would you react?

A) By visualising the word "apple" in your head.

B) By saying the word out loud to yourself.

C) By imagining things related to apples (cores, pips, trees, etc).

9. You're in a new place for the first time and need directions. What would you do?

A) Find a map and follow it.

B) Ask someone for directions.

C) Keep walking around until you find the location for yourself.

10. When you meet a new person, what do you remember the most?

A) Their face.

B) Their name.

C) What you did with them, or what you talked about.

Now that you've finished, you can find out what kind of learner you are.

- **If most of your answers were A**, then you are a visual learner. You learn by using your eyes to analyse diagrams and notes.

- **If most of your answers were B**, then you are an aural learner. Spoken words sink in best, so you do well when listening to yourself or others.

- **If most of your answers were C**, then you are a kinaesthetic learner. You study best when getting involved and doing things for yourself, rather than watching or listening.

Remember that you don't necessarily have to fall into just one of these three categories. A wide range of learning methods might work for you, so it's good to keep experimenting to find out which techniques suit you best.

In the next few sections, we will cover the three main styles of learning, so you can get some top tips on how to study efficiently!

Visual Learning

Visual learning is exactly as it sounds – you learn by visually representing information, or by having information visually represented for you. This can involve pages of notes, mind-maps, tables, animations, slideshows and more. All of these can be used to make information easy to digest visually.

While modern computers are adept at note-taking and mind-map making, you might find it more helpful to ditch the laptop for a while and use a pen and paper. This way, you can improve your handwriting skills, make notes which are available at any time, as well as avoid distractions which come too easily whilst on a computer connected to the internet!

Visual learning is excellent for any subject that has a lot of written text to digest. This applies to everything from English to the sciences, where a passage of information needs to be dissected to find the most important parts. Note-taking can condense a whole chapter of dates, facts and figures into a page or two. Mind-maps are a great way of connecting loads of key facts to a single core concept, such as an event or an important person. Additionally, videos and slideshows are excellent for representing data in a clear manner.

Visual learners tend to be good at remembering images and charts. They'll likely find it easier to remember details of pictures and photographs, and might perform well in memory games where they have to spot which object has been removed from a collection. For this reason, visual learners are suited to organising their revision materials into diagrams, which they will likely find easy to remember.

At A-Level, you'll have a huge amount of information that you need to retain for the exams, regardless of what subject you take. Some of the following visual learning techniques, such as note-taking and mind-maps, are excellent for holding onto large amounts of facts.

Note-taking and Summarisation

This method is exactly as it sounds: you write down notes based on the information in your textbooks or lesson materials. The goal is to collect all of the vital information from your resources. Use the following steps to take notes effectively:

1. Read through your textbook and other learning materials once, without making notes. Do this so that you get an overall understanding of the material.

2. Go back to the start of the material and begin to re-write the key details in your own words. Alternatively, if the book belongs to you, you can underline key points.

3. Continue re-writing important details until you've finished a whole chapter. Make sure to organise the bullet points into sections.

4. Once finished, read over your notes.

5. Then, turn your pages of notes over so you can't see them, then try to remember as much as possible.

6. Repeat this until you're able to remember all of your notes without reading them.

How you go about writing these notes will depend on what you're studying and which techniques best suit you. One way to help notes stick in your head is to underline the key words from sentences in your text books or other materials. Once you've done that, you can lay them out in your notes. This is beneficial because it separates the important details from the less important ones. For example:

> *"One of the <u>key themes</u> of William Shakespeare's 'Othello' is <u>jealousy</u>. <u>Iago warns Othello</u> of jealousy being a "<u>green-eyed monster</u>," and ultimately <u>it's Iago's exploitation of Othello's jealousy</u> that leads to <u>Othello's downfall</u>."*

By underlining all of the key information, we can now organise the facts from the above paragraph into something easier to remember:

- *Key theme = jealousy*

- *Iago warns Othello of "green-eyed monster"*

- *Iago exploits Othello's jealousy*

- *This results in Othello's downfall*

This method allows you to organise information succinctly, so when you return to read it later, you can absorb the vital facts and leave everything else out. By limiting yourself to these facts, you can focus on the details which are necessary. This is useful because you don't want to overload your brain with long, clunky sentences; when all you need is the important stuff. What's important is that you transfer the notes into an easily digestible format.

For longer pieces of text with more vital information, you may need to write notes in full sentences. This can be a great way to improve your handwriting and writing skills. The other beneficial part of this method comes in the form of re-writing the information in your own words. It may be tempting to fall into the habit of copying information word-for-word, and you might find yourself doing this without even thinking about it. If you're doing this, you're probably not internalising the information, and you might not even understand it properly. There are plenty of machines capable of copying things exactly, but that doesn't mean that they understand the information that they're making copies of! So, you should prove that you understand what you're reading by turning it into your own words. For example:

> "One of the key themes of William Shakespeare's 'Othello' is jealousy. Iago warns Othello of jealousy being a "green-eyed monster," and ultimately it's Iago's exploitation of Othello's jealousy that leads to Othello's downfall."

This could become:

> "Jealousy is the main theme of 'Othello'. In the play, Iago warns Othello that jealousy is a "green-eyed monster". In the end, Iago takes advantage of Othello's jealous nature and this results in Othello's downfall."

Here, the content of both texts remains largely the same. However, by writing the work in your own words, you are demonstrating to yourself that you have identified the key parts of the text and understood them. Writing information in your own words is a great way to test your comprehension of the text; if you're able to sum up the message of the paragraph in your own words, then you probably understand its content quite well.

Note: Check with your teacher before underlining or writing in textbooks. If the book doesn't belong to you, it's likely that you won't be allowed to write in it!

Although writing notes allows you to read over them later, the key part of this process is writing them in the first place. When you turn notes from a text into your own writing, you're committing it to memory. Reading it afterwards may be helpful in the short-term, but actually writing it sinks into your head more easily, and it's more likely to become part of your long-term memory.

Visual learners also benefit from making their work more vibrant and striking. This can be done by using different text sizes or colours. For instance, you could write more important words in larger text so that they stand out more. So, when you return to read your notes, you'll see the vital details immediately.

"Jealousy is the main theme of 'Othello'. In the play, Iago warns Othello that jealousy is a "green-eyed monster". In the end, Iago takes advantage of Othello's jealous nature and this results in Othello's downfall."

Different colours could represent different things in your work. For example, if you were given a text including the pros and cons of nuclear energy, you could highlight the positive parts in green and the negative parts in red. Then, you could use a colour such as amber (or orange) to show important details which aren't necessarily positive or negative.

This traffic light system can be used in all sorts of ways. If you were reading a poem for English Literature, you might notice different themes. The main (most important) themes could be highlighted in green, less important themes can be highlighted in amber and then the least important themes could be highlighted in red.

Finally, you can write your notes as tables if it suits the topic. This is particularly useful for making note of 'for and against' parts of your course. For example, a student revising for Religious Studies might make use of the following:

Euthanasia: For or Against?

For	Against
It gives individuals the chance to die with dignity and relatively little suffering	The right to die might turn into the "duty" to die at a certain age to prevent strain on health services
Legal euthanasia treats individuals as sensible people with personal liberty	In some cases, the individual might not be in control of their mental faculties and might not understand the situation properly
Less terminally-ill people in hospitals will free-up resources for people who can be treated and/or cured	Potentially de-values human beings just because they are ill, might make society less willing to help the elderly and terminally-ill

Prevents a terminally-ill person from becoming an emotional strain on the entire family	One could argue that it's against God's will to end someone's life

Note-taking is a great technique for any kind of learner to make use of, but it's certainly most beneficial for visual learners. For some people, note-taking is the foundation for all of their revision, and they use other activities to simply break up huge chunks of writing notes over and over. It can certainly be monotonous, but it's a tried-and-tested method that lots of students have made use of.

Note-taking: Pros and Cons

Pros	Cons
Simple and often effective	Can be a strain on the hands after long periods of writing
Doesn't require anything other than a pen, paper, and textbooks	Can be incredibly monotonous
Can be used to practise handwriting as well	
Leaves you with pages of notes that you can read more casually	
Re-writing information shows you understand it better	

Mind-Maps

Another great way of visually representing your notes, is by creating mind-maps. These are webs of ideas and information connected to each other, to show how they are related. Generally, a central concept appears in the centre of a page, and then other details spread away from it. This is excellent for quickly jotting down all of the information you can remember, and then organising it into sections. Take a look at the following example:

Mind Map - *Othello*

- The foundation of Othello and Desdemona's relationship is passion, not love

- Othello believes that love in marriage takes time to develop

- Desdemona's platonic love to Cassio is misinterpreted by Othello as sexual love

- Desdemona's father sees Othello marrying Desdemona as theft of some kind of property

- The mixed-race marriage between Othello and Desdemona would've been unusual and likely the target of prejudice and scrutiny

- The two married women in the play (Desdemona and Emilia) are wrongfully accused of adultery

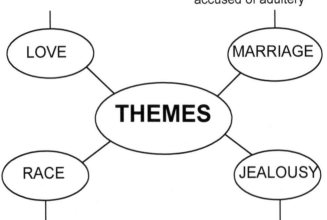

- Othello is a black man in a high position in the Venetian military, which would have been unusual for the time

- Iago uses suspicions about Othello and Desdemona's mixed-race marriage to his advantage

- Othello has internalised some of this racial prejudice, believing himself to be unworthy of Desdemona's love

- Iago warns Othello of jealousy being a "green-eyed monster"

- Iago himself has experienced jealousy via his relationship with Emilia

- Othello's jealousy clouds his judgement, despite him once being a calm and collected individual

Mind-Maps: Pros and Cons

Pros	Cons
Can be made by hand or on a computer	Not effective for some subjects, such as Maths
If done by hand, can be a great way of improving handwriting	Has the potential to be less efficient and more time consuming than other methods such as note-taking
Forces you to write incredibly concise notes, which is great for remembering	Not necessarily an excellent method if you aren't particularly creative
Excellent for subjects with lots of connected events or concepts	
Allows you to be creative which can alleviate some stress	
Excellent for memory since you can visually recall the entire mind map in your head	

Videos, Animations and Slideshows

Visual learners can benefit greatly from watching videos and animations to help them revise. There's a wealth of videos online, often made by people who recently sat exams, which can be used to help you get a better grasp of the material. Head over to a popular video-sharing website such as YouTube and search for the topic you're currently revising. Always double-check that the information that they give is correct and relevant (by comparing what the videos say to what's in your own textbooks), because it's possible that these people studied a different curriculum to you.

Watching videos created by people who didn't write your textbooks is great for some subjects because it may offer alternative opinions and viewpoints. This is especially useful for essay-based subjects such as English Literature, History, and Religious Studies, where having a range of interpretations and different opinions at your disposal can flesh out your answers even further. This is less important for other subjects such as the sciences or Maths, but nevertheless these videos still serve their function of being interesting to the eye.

Outside of the usual video-sharing sites, there are plenty of online resources which will give you videos, animations and slideshows to help you get your head around whatever you're currently revising. Again, remember to check that the information you're receiving matches what's in your textbooks.

This method is great for splitting up long sessions of note-taking. If you've spent the whole day revising, and you're getting tired of writing down notes, watching some revision videos online might provide some relief.

Note: watching videos online can be an excellent way of revising, but make sure that you stay on topic. It's far too easy to get distracted by everything else on the internet (e.g. social media, online games) – stay focused!

Visual Aids: Pros and Cons

Pros	Cons
Can be interesting or even funny to watch, and this can help ideas stick in your brain	Access to the internet can lead to easy distractions if you don't exercise self-restraint
Can give you an insight on alternative arguments and points of view	Sometimes the content in the videos won't completely match your school curriculum – some things might not be relevant
Works as a good break from more intensive revision activities	

Am I a Visual Learner?

Do you find that you can recall information based on how it's displayed on a page? Try taking some notes or making a mind-map based on resources in your textbooks, then turn the paper over and try and re-write the notes. Once you've re-written everything, flip the original page back over and see how well you did at remembering it all. If you could remember most or all of it, that probably means that you can learn from visual aids.

Aural Learning

Aural learning is all about listening, both to your own voice and others. Aural learners absorb information by listening to it being said, either by themselves or by others. While it only really involves your ears, aural learning is incredibly flexible. There are plenty of ways to revise effectively if you are an aural learner.

Aural learning is excellent for subjects which have lots of short, sweet bits of information. For example, visual learners will likely write the process down as a series of bullet points, or perhaps a flow chart, whilst aural learners will want to listen to each of these points individually, to allow them to sink in.

Reading Out Loud

This is the simplest method of aural learning, and can be done on your own and without any extra equipment. All you need is yourself, your textbook (or other study materials) and your voice!

Start by opening on a chapter or paragraph that you're comfortable with, and then begin to read it to yourself out loud. When you come across a sentence or point which might be more complicated or confusing, read it multiple times. By doing this, it will stick in your head more, making you more likely to remember it.

Aural learners can benefit from using certain tones

for different points. Singing notes that you need to remember, or creating catchy rhymes for them, can help you to keep them in mind more easily. It might sound silly at first, but they can be incredibly useful.

Aural learners can create acrostics and mnemonics to help them remember difficult spellings or more complex ideas. Acrostics and mnemonics are almost opposites of one another. An acrostic is a phrase you keep in mind to remember lots of smaller phrases or information.

For example, BIDMAS is an acrostic which can be used to remember how you should go about solving maths questions:

Brackets

Indices (or 'powers of')

Division

Multiplication

Addition

Subtraction

Mnemonics, on the other hand, are a collection of words used to remember a single, larger word. These are particularly good for spellings:

BECAUSE = **B**ig **E**lephants **C**an't **A**lways **U**se **S**mall **E**xits

The colours in the rainbow can be remembered using the following mnemonic:

ROYGBIV = **R**ichard **O**f **Y**ork **G**ave **B**attle **I**n **V**ain

You can also use this acrostic to help you remember the colours of the rainbow!

Red

Orange

Yellow

Green

Blue

Indigo

Violet

Aural leaners can repeat the phrase "ROYGBIV" or "Richard of York gave battle in vain" until it sinks in fully. Then, if you got stuck in a test, all you'd need to do is recall the phrase!

Of course, the content at A-Level will be much more complicated than "ROYGBIV" or the spelling of "because". However, these exercises can still be used to remember key formulae and phrases.

Note: any kind of learner can make use of acrostics and mnemonics. Even if you aren't an aural learner, try them yourself!

Reading Out Loud: Pros and Cons

Pros	Cons
Requires very little equipment to get started	Requires a specific environment – a place where you're on your own and can speak out loud
Acrostics and other rhymes are bite-sized, meaning you can try remembering them on the go	Can eventually get tiring
Great for making sure you're actually reading the material and taking it in	
Has the potential for self-recording (see below)	

Self-recording

For this technique, all you need is your voice, some reading material and a device which you can record yourself with. In the past, you would have had to use a specific device called a dictation machine to record yourself. Nowadays, almost any modern smartphone or tablet has voice recording capabilities. So long as it has a microphone, it should be able to record your voice as well. If these options aren't available, dictation machines aren't too expensive, and they might be worth the investment.

Note: Many laptops can record your voice too. If it has a camera, it's probably capable of recording your voice with its microphone!

If you've chosen to use the "reading aloud" method of revision, you might as well record yourself at the same time. The self-recording technique is quite simple; all you need to do is record yourself reading your notes.

The great thing about this method is that both recording and listening help you to remember information. While you're reading your notes out loud into the microphone, you're going to be committing them to memory, just like you would when reading out loud. Once you're done reading all of them, you can listen to them through speakers or headphones whenever you're studying.

Here are some tips to make your recordings even easier to study from:

• Make sure you're not speaking too close to the microphone, or too far away from it. Do a couple of test runs to make sure your microphone is working properly.

• Speak slowly and clearly, so that you can listen back easily.

• Place emphasis on the more important details in your notes. Try changing your tone of voice for certain key phrases or facts, so that they stick out more.

• When you're done recording, send the files to your phone or smart device so that they're always handy.

Whenever you have a free 10 minutes or so, you can listen to your notes!

Self-recording: Pros and Cons

Pros	Cons
Has all of the benefits of reading out loud	Requires some kind of recording device, might take a while to set up
Allows you to listen back to your recordings later on	

Podcasts and other Recordings

If you don't like hearing your own voice, or don't have a way to record yourself, there are still plenty of resources that you can listen to. Revision podcasts are easily accessible, and quite often free to download and listen to. There are also plenty of resources on YouTube (such as CareerVidz) and other video-sharing websites, which you can listen to via smartphones, computers and tablets.

Remember to make sure that the revision materials are relevant. Depending on the exam board, the topics that you learn may differ. Before listening to a revision podcast, double check that the topics match those in your textbook or syllabus. If you're unsure of where to start, ask your teacher if they know of any resources that may be relevant.

Like self-recording, revision podcasts and other materials are useful because you can carry them with you at any time, with the help of smartphones and tablets. This means that, wherever you are, you can put a bit of time into listening to them.

Another bonus of these techniques is that they can be far less tiring. Reading out loud from a textbook or writing pages upon pages of notes can get incredibly boring, especially after long sessions. Using revision podcasts can often be a slightly more fun way of learning – so make use of it when you aren't feeling entirely up to more formal revision.

Advice for Parents

If you have access to your child's syllabus, find out what exam boards their exams are on. Depending on the board, the topics will differ, and so some resources (such as revision guides and podcasts) won't be as relevant. If you are unsure of the exam boards that your child's exams are on, get in touch with your child's school to find out. Bear in mind that exam boards may differ per subject. So, try and get a list of all your child's subjects and their respective exam boards.

Podcasts and Recordings: Pros and Cons

Pros	Cons
Can be used as a break from doing your own revision	Sometimes exact material in the podcast might not match your curriculum
Can offer alternative ideas and opinions which strengthen your own knowledge	Require some kind of device (e.g. smartphone, tablet, computer or mp3 player) to listen to them
Can be stored on a phone or mp3 player and listened to anywhere	
Often free of charge	

Discussing With Others

Many revision techniques can be quite lonely. Sometimes, it's nice to have a bit of human interaction. Thankfully, aural learners can make use of discussion with a revision partner. This is a great revision method if you have a friend or family member available to help. All this involves is sitting (or standing!) with your revision partner and going through the material with them. There are two different ways in which you could do this:

- **Ask and answer questions.** With this method, your revision partner will hold the textbook in front of themselves for them to read, and then ask questions about the material. It's your job to answer them as accurately as possible. If you get the answer correct, congratulations! Move onto the next one. If you answer incorrectly, your revision partner can steer you in the right direction by revealing a bit more information, such as the first letter of the word, or some related details.

If your revision partner is a classmate, then you should try and take turns asking and answering questions. By doing this, you're both being exposed to the material and can get things done quickly.

- **Open discussion.** This method involves you and your revision partner speaking freely about the material. If your partner is also studying for an exam, both of you should try to discuss without looking at your textbooks or notes. However, keep the books close-by in case both of you can't remember something, or are unsure of precise details. It's also a good idea to share notes too, so that you can make sure that you've got something correct.

If your revision partner isn't studying for the exam (such as a family member), allow them to have the book open in front of them, but so that you can't see it. Then, just speak to them about the things that you're revising, and they can fact-check you along the way.

Both of these methods are great ways to learn with a partner, and are excellent ways of making sure that your other revision techniques are working. Discussing with a partner is most beneficial later on during revision, when you've already learned lots of information by yourself, and just want to test your ability to remember it.

> **Note: Thanks to modern phones and internet, you don't even need to sit in the same room as your revision partner in order to revise. There are plenty of communication apps and programs that you can download to your phone, tablet or computer which will let you revise with friends.**

Discussing with Others: Pros and Cons

Pros	Cons
It's a fantastic way of remembering information, as well as finding out what you know and where you need to improve	Can be difficult to organise, particularly outside of school hours
Benefits two people (you and your revision partner)	It's possible to get distracted and chat about irrelevant things!
It's a great way for parents and family members to get involved in the revision process	

Am I an Aural Learner?

Aural learners tend to focus on what they are hearing and saying more than what they are seeing and doing. If you think this applies to you, give some of the above styles a try. Aural learning is especially useful for those who struggle to sit down and take notes for longer periods of time, and the above techniques can be used by anyone who wants to mix up their revision.

Kinaesthetic Learning

Kinaesthetic learning is all about *doing*, rather than looking or hearing. Kinaesthetic learners shouldn't limit themselves to sitting in one place and trying to write pages full of notes. Instead, they should be finding more creative and unconventional ways of learning. There's a huge range of techniques for a kinaesthetic learner to tap into!

Since kinaesthetic learning is such a broad field, it can apply to almost any subject and any kind of information. If you think you might be a kinaesthetic learner, give some of the following techniques a try.

Flashcards

With flashcards, you'll want to write down some key notes from your textbooks or other revision materials. Take a large piece of card and cut it up into smaller segments. On one side of each card, write down the word or concept that you need to remember the meaning of. On the other, write down the key facts associated with the word. Here's an example to get you started:

Front	Reverse
Sonnet	A fourteen-line poem which is written in iambic pentameter. Uses specific rhyme scheme. Has a single, focused theme.

Front and **Reverse** labels appear above the table.

Once you've written all of your flashcards, turn them all facing front up and sort them into a deck (like a deck of playing cards). Then, take each card, read out the main word on the front, and then try and recall as many of the key facts as possible. You can do this by reading out loud, or by reading in your head – whichever suits you best.

Once you think you've finished listing them all, flip the card over to see if you missed any details. If you didn't, congratulations! Put the card to one side and save it for later. If you missed anything, take note of it and put the card back at the bottom of the deck. This means that, once you've got through all of the other cards, you can attempt the ones you couldn't completely remember before. One by one, you'll start to eliminate cards from the deck, since you'll remember all of the details for each of them. Once you've completed them all, take a short break before trying again.

Another method for using cards is to stick them around your workspace. Write a note on each piece of card and leave it somewhere in your room where you're likely to see it often. Stick some to your mirror or the edge of a laptop screen, or even place them on the wall or on a bookshelf. You can even leave them around your house so that whenever you stop to make yourself a snack or go to the toilet, you'll still be revising!

Advice for Parents

If your child finds placing notes quite effective, it's worth letting them place cards around the house. Let your child place the notes wherever its safe and useful for them to do so.

Flash Cards: Pros and Cons

Pros	Cons
A pack of small cards is portable, so flashcards can be used wherever you are	Can take a while to put together (writing on individual cards, etc)
They're incredibly useful for learning key terms and their meanings	
Writing them in the first place helps commit ideas to memory	

Multitasking

Multitasking simply involves doing another activity whilst doing your ordinary revision. By doing this, you'll start to associate certain facts with the things you do. If you enjoy exercise, try listening to recordings of yourself reading out notes, while going for a run or working out in some other way. If you play video games, stop and test yourself on a question every so often. This probably won't work as a main revision technique, but it's a way to do some light revision on a day off, or once you've finished the bulk of your studying for the evening.

Multitasking: Pros and Cons

Pros	Cons
Bite-sized but effective	Doesn't really work as a main revision technique
Can be done anywhere and at any time	
More light-hearted than intense revision sessions	

Learning Games

For this technique, you're probably going to need access to either the internet or dedicated workbooks. You'll want to find games or other interactive tools which involve *doing* things rather than just reading them. For example, one game might require you to match up key words to their meanings, or key dates to the events which occurred on them. You can actually do this one yourself, in the same way that you made flashcards. Cut up a large piece of paper in separate pieces, and then on half of them write a key word. Then write something related to each key word on all of the other pieces. Shuffle up all of the cards, then try to match them up.

You should also check online for other learning games. As always, double check that the content of the games matches what you're learning in class, so you don't confuse yourself.

Learning Games: Pros and Cons

Pros	Cons
Entertaining and highly effective for kinaesthetic learners	Online learning games aren't always easy to find
Work as a great break from more intensive revision methods	Creating your own learning games can be time-consuming
Can be an excellent way to revise with others	

Am I a Kinaesthetic Learner?

If you find yourself *doing* things rather than reading or listening, then kinaesthetic learning might be the style for you. You might find that it's much easier for you to do something for yourself, rather than ask someone to explain it to you. You might also find that you work best in unconventional settings: maybe you work better while exercising than sitting at a desk.

Looking Back on Your GCSEs

In the last book in this series, *How to Pass Your GCSEs With Level 9s*, we pointed out that GCSEs are a great testing ground for revision styles and techniques. While A-Levels are different to GCSEs in many ways, and they demand more from you, you can learn from previous years of studying for exams. Consider the following:

• What revision techniques worked best for you at GCSE level? How can you apply them to A-Level?

• What didn't work so well? Is it worth giving it another try?

Feel free to experiment with learning styles and revision techniques, but don't be afraid to go back to what suits you best. Sometimes, being in your comfort zone is just what you need in order to perform well.

A Final Word about Learning Styles

The techniques explored here are only a few of the many ways you can learn and revise effectively. Start by experimenting with the methods we've listed, but feel free to branch out and try your own ways of revising. Different people think and work differently to one another, and so you need to find your own unique way of learning that works best for you. Remember that, just because you may believe that you have a specific learning style, you don't have to stick to a limited range of techniques. Be creative and give everything a try – it's the only way to truly know what works best for you.

Starting Your Revision

So far, you've had an overview of what A-Levels are, an introduction to different styles of learning, and a detailed look at many revision techniques that can be used at A-Level. In this chapter, we'll be shifting the focus slightly, and taking a look at other skills and tricks to help you prepare for your A-Levels. These include:

- How to create a revision timetable;

- How to keep yourself motivated;

- How to prevent yourself from becoming distracted;

- How to avoid cramming;

- How to make use of past papers and mark schemes.

Revision Timetables and Planning

Now that you've had the opportunity to explore the different ways of learning, it's time to turn the focus to other general aspects of revision: creating and sticking to a timetable, and making full use of revision materials. Both are extremely valuable when revising, and proper handling of both will improve your grade and make you more likely to score high in exams and in controlled assessments.

The goal of having a revision timetable is to map out all of the work that needs to be done in the time after you've started, up until your exams begin. Your plan doesn't need to be expertly crafted or even particularly nice to look at; it just needs to be clear and easy to read.

The first thing you should do is list every subject that you are taking exams in. Once you've done that, try and find every topic or module within that subject.

For example, a breakdown of AS level Biology may look like this:

1. Molecules

    • Polymers;

    • Carbohydrates;

    • Lipids;

    • Proteins;

    • DNA.

2. Cells

    • The structure of cells;

    • The structure of viruses;

    • Cell membranes;

    • The immune system.

3. Organisms and their environment

    • Surface area to volume ratio;

    • Gas exchange;

    • Digestion;

    • Mass transport.

4. Genetic information

    • DNA, genes and chromosomes;

- Protein synthesis;

- Genetic diversity;

- Taxonomy and Species;

- Biodiversity.

You may wish to go into slightly more detail for each of the topics, but as a foundation, this will be enough to fill in a revision timetable. Do this for every module and for every subject, so that you know roughly how much material there is to cover. It's also worth taking a look at how long each of the chapters for these modules are in your textbook, so that you're aware of any abnormally large or small topics.

Once you've done this, it's time to prioritise all of your subjects and topics. Some people like to rank all their subjects from most important to least important. In other words, it might be worth considering which subjects you find more difficult, and giving them higher priority. If you already feel quite confident about a certain part of your studies, place it slightly lower on your list. This means that the areas that need the most attention will receive it.

Once you've prioritised your subjects, you can also prioritise modules. Bear in mind that a lot of topics in many subjects are cumulative – which means that a good understanding of earlier modules is vital for getting to grips with later ones. This is especially the case with Maths and Science, where you're building up knowledge as you go along. For these ones, it's better to start at the beginning and work your way through, but other subjects might allow you to mix things up a bit.

Your timetable should include all of the material that you need to revise outside of school hours. The best way to find out what you need to cover, is to take a look at how your textbooks divide their content, and then use those to fill the timetable. You'll be treated to some blank templates for a timetable at the end of this book. The following example timetable shows what a single week of revision during term-time may look like. Take a look at this timetable to get an idea of how to organise your time:

	Monday	Tuesday	Wednesday	Thursday	Friday	Saturday	Sunday
09:00 AM-10:00AM	School	School	School	School	School	Biology - Digestion	Biology - Mock Exam
10:00 AM -11:00 AM	School	School	School	School	School	Biology - Mass Transport	Biology - Mark Shceme
11:00 AM -12:00 PM	School	School	School	School	School	Biology - DNA	Biology - Free Revision
12:00 PM - 01:00PM	School	School	School	School	School	Biology - Protein Synthesis	Biology - Free Revision
01:00 PM - 02:00 PM	School	School	School	School	School	Biology - Genetic Diversity	Bliology - Free Revision

	Monday	Tuesday	Wednesday	Thursday	Friday	Saturday	Sunday
02:00 PM - 03:00 PM	School	School	School	School	School	Biology - Digestion	Biology - Mock Exam
03:00 PM - 04:00 PM	Break	Break	Break	Break	Break	Break	Break
04:00 PM - 05:00 PM	Biology - Polymers	Biology - Proteins	Biology - Cell Structure	Biology - Cell Membrane	Biology - Surface to Volume Ratio	Biology - Biodiversity	Eng Lit - Free Revision
05:00 PM - 06:00PM	Biology - Carbohy-drates	Biology - DNA	Biology - Virus Structure	Biology - The Immune System	Biology - Gas Exchange	Eng Lit - Reading Poetry	Eng Lit - Free Revision
06:00 PM - 07:00 PM	Biology - Lipids	Eng Lit - Reading Poetry	Eng Lit - Reading Shakespeare	Eng Lit - Reading Poetry	Eng Lit - Revising Quotes	Eng Lit - Reading Poetry	Eng Lit - Free Revision

Remember to factor in breaks and school time. During term time, you're going to be in school for most of the day, only giving you a couple of hours in the afternoon and evening. Naturally, you're going to feel more tired in the evenings after school than at the weekends, so you might find that doing the bulk of your revision on Saturday and Sunday is helpful.

On the other hand, you might want to do all of your revision during the week, then have relatively little to do at the weekend. Spend the first two weeks of your revision trying out some different routines, find out what works best for you, then stick to one for the duration of the exam season.

During the school holidays, the game changes entirely. All of a sudden you don't have to go to school for 6 hours a day, meaning that you have a lot more time on your hands. While you may want to take a break from everything, you should make use of all the free time you have during these breaks. In fact, many students do the bulk of their revision during these holidays. Of course, you should take some time off, but make sure you take advantage of the holiday period. This can really put you ahead for the next term.

How Do I Motivate Myself?

Getting motivated to revise in the first place can be incredibly difficult, and requires a lot of determination and self-control. The earlier you start your revision, the better, but you'll probably be tempted to put off revision: "I'll start next week", or "it's way too early to start revising."

Try to start revising 8 weeks before your first exam. This should give you plenty of time to get through all of your topics.

However, even starting the process can be a pain, and when the exams are so far away it's difficult to get the ball rolling. So, you need to motivate yourself to start revising as early and as well as possible. In this section, we'll take a look at some of the ways you can keep yourself motivated and make sure you get through your revision.

Revision Styles

Start by finding revision styles that you actually enjoy. This might sound ridiculous, but if you can find a few techniques that aren't completely unbearable, you'll be more willing to make a start with revision. Remember that you don't have to be constantly doing 'hard revision' such as note-taking. Mix things up and try a number of styles to keep things fresh early on, then maybe move into something more serious later.

Ease Into It

Before you start, revision can feel like a huge mountain, impossible to climb to the top of. It can be incredibly daunting. You might be overwhelmed by the feeling that you are completely unprepared and don't know enough. That said, you need to make a start sometime. Some revision is better than no revision at all, so if you're struggling to get started with your studies, ease your way into it. Start by revising for a much shorter period of time, and maybe focus on the things that you already know well or most enjoy. Once you're comfortable and confident, move onto something that you're less sure of.

Treat Yourself

Make sure you keep yourself motivated with some treats. You don't need to go overboard, but the "carrot and stick" method of revision can keep you working for longer periods of time, allowing you to get through more work. Things like "I'll get some ice cream, but only after I've done the next 3 pages" are a great way of keeping you going and keeping your spirits up.

Think Ahead

Finally, always think ahead past exams. Life continues after your A-Levels, and you'll be treated to an extra-long summer once you've finished. You might feel that you're not in a great place while revising, that your social life is suffering or your free time is being eaten up by studies, but it will all be worth it when you get great results. This positive outlook – thinking towards the future – is one of the best ways to get you started with revision, and keep you going with it too.

Staying Focused

Sometimes, revision can be a total pain, and you'd rather do anything (even sit around doing absolutely nothing!) than open a book and do some hard learning. It's very tempting to procrastinate, but falling into the trap of putting off revision is one of the biggest mistakes you can possibly do.

<u>Here are our top 5 tips for avoiding procrastination and getting on with your work!</u>

1. Turn Off Distractions

The first thing you should do before starting a revision session is remove any distractions from your workspace. The biggest offenders for distracting pupils are games consoles, social media, mobile phones, and of course television. The simple solution to this is to turn off these devices, and put them somewhere out of view or reach, so you aren't tempted to turn them back on and continue texting, messaging or playing games.

Sometimes, however, it isn't practical to move all of these devices. In this case, it's better to find a new workspace, free of electronic devices and other distractions. Many people find that their kitchen or dining room table is an excellent place to study, but find what works best for you and your home. If there's nowhere in your house that's suitable for studying, the local library may be a good choice.

<u>When choosing a place to study, consider the following:</u>

- Is it quiet?

- Are there any gadgets to distract you?

- Will people be walking in and out of the room? Will that distract you?

- Is it comfortable?

- Is there plenty of room for you and all of your notes?

Things get a little trickier when you're using computerised or other online resources such as revision games or podcasts. In these cases, you're going to need your computer, phone or tablet with you, so you'll need to exercise some self-control. Log yourself out of social media if you feel that it's necessary to do so, and make sure to turn off notifications for messaging apps on your phone. You can always take a look during your breaks.

Finally, a few words about listening to music while revising. Be very careful when playing music (especially music with lyrics) while studying. It works for some people, but others will find it incredibly distracting. Experiment with it for yourself, but if you find that it doesn't help you, promptly turn it off.

2. Give Yourself Plenty of Breaks (but not too many!)

Believe it or not, one of the best ways to avoid procrastination is to take regular breaks. Concentration tends to slide after 45 minutes for a lot of teenagers, so don't push yourself to revise for longer periods of time. If you do this, you'll likely get distracted by almost everything around you, or just get bored or tired. The solution to this problem is to place regular breaks after every chunk of time spent revising. So, if you revise for 45 minutes, you should give yourself a 10 or 15-minute break afterwards. Start with this and then adjust it as necessary, until you get into a routine which is comfortable for you. Remember not to go overboard with breaks. Make sure that you stick to your timetable and routine, so that a 15-minute break doesn't turn into an hour spent watching TV!

3. Stick to Your Revision Timetable

Writing and filling in a revision timetable is one thing, but it's another thing entirely to stick to it throughout your entire exam season. If it helps, make your timetable more detailed to include breaks and other activities.

It can be tempting to put off revision or bargain with yourself: "I'll only do 2 hours today but I'll make up for it tomorrow," or "I don't really need to know this stuff, I'll take the rest of the day off." Both of these are risky mind-sets, which don't put you in a great place for succeeding. Good organisation skills come in handy here, and you should try and keep to your timetable as much as possible.

Of course, you can be flexible with your time. Sometimes things come up, and you shouldn't completely sacrifice your social life during the revision period. Just make sure it's reasonable, though.

4. Make Your Working Environment Comfortable

Outside of keeping things quiet and free from distracting gadgets, you should make sure that your revision space is comfortable enough for you to work in. If the room is too cold or hot, or your chair isn't comfortable to sit on, then you might find yourself not wanting to revise. Make sure your revision space is as comfortable as possible.

Advice for Parents

Ask your child if they like their revision space. If they don't, find out what the problem is and try to help them solve it.

5. Mix Things Up

The final tip for staying focused is to mix things up every so often. One way to do this, is to change the subject that you're revising halfway through the day. This means that you'll still be revising, and you'll keep things fresh. You don't need to switch it up too often, but when you find yourself getting too bored of a topic to continue, finish it and then move onto something else entirely, preferably an area from another subject.

You could also change your revision techniques from time to time, to keep things interesting. If you've spent the whole morning writing notes, why not switch over to a podcast or some learning games? You can refer back to our section on different learning styles to get some ideas on how to make your revision more varied.

Cramming

Cramming is the act of trying to stuff in as much revision as possible in the days (or even hours!) just before the exam. It's also possibly the biggest act of sabotage that you can do to yourself.

Cramming happens when a pupil either does very little or no revision before the exams. Before they know it, the exam dates have crept up on them, sending them into a state of panic. These pupils tend to then rush through their textbooks and materials, trying to cover weeks' worth of work in just a few days. In almost every case, this is simply not enough time to adequately revise everything. So, people who cram very rarely benefit from it.

Cramming can actually worsen your performance in an exam. Students who cram often find themselves completely blanking on information when they start answering questions, leaving them helpless during an exam. Cramming doesn't work because you aren't giving your brain enough time to let information sink in.

In an ideal world, you should try to finish your revision for a subject 2 or 3 days before the exam starts. This doesn't always go to plan, but aim to have your revision finished at least 2 days before. Revising the night before an exam is a bad idea, and you should avoid doing so. The day before your exam (and in the hours leading up to it as well) should be spent relaxing and keeping calm, eating well and not allowing yourself to become stressed out by looming thoughts about the test. If you get to the day before your exam and you've finished everything, then you've done an excellent job, and deserve an evening to relax.

Advice for Parents

Keep an eye on your child's revision schedule, and every so often check that they're on top of their work. You don't want to intrude too much, but a subtle reminder might make sure that your child doesn't let their exams creep up on them.

Using Mock Exams and Practice Questions

Once you're well into your revision, you'll find that you've got lots of information swimming around in your head. When you feel like you're getting to this point, it may be time to attempt a mock exam. These are excellent ways of testing how much you already know, and it also gives you an insight into what you still need to do in order to ace your exams.

Mock exams are so useful that some people use them and no other techniques when revising. This isn't strictly advised – it's better that you start by revising your notes before trying a mock test, mainly because you may not know enough or remember enough to fully complete a mock exam.

How Do I Find Mock Exams?

Finding mock exams is usually quite easy. The first port of call is your school or your teacher. It's possible that they have some mock exams already printed to give to you. If they don't, then it might be worth suggesting that they make some available for yourself and other students.

If your teacher doesn't have any mock exams prepared, try and find out as much about the exam(s) you want to revise for before looking up papers. You need to find out the following before looking up past papers:

- Your exam board – you'll probably need to go to their website to find accurate past papers;

- The name of your specification – sometimes there are 'A' and 'B' versions of the same subject, offered as separate courses (e.g. "Biology A" and "Biology B");

- The year that you'll be sitting your exams – specifications tend to change every few years and that means some older past papers might be irrelevant.

The easiest resources to access are past papers, or actual exams from previous years. These are free to download from exam board websites and can be read from your computer screen, or printed off so that you can write on them.

In addition, there are plenty of workbooks specific to your subjects, which will include practice papers and sample questions.

Printing pages upon pages of past papers can get expensive, but it can be a vital way to learn where your strengths lie and where you need to improve. A solution which will allow you to take advantage of mock papers, as well as save you money on printer ink, is to find settings on your printer such as 'draft' or 'ink saver' mode. These will print the past papers out in a slightly lower quality, but usually the papers are still entirely useable.

How Should I Use Mock Exams?

There are two different ways to use mock exams in your revision. The first way is to attempt a full mock exam as you work through topics of the subject. For example, say that you have a Science exam with three different sections. One of these sections is on evolution and adaptation, the next is on the human anatomy, and the final section is about how drugs and other substances can have an effect on the body. You figure out that these are the three topics you need to learn, so you go through past papers online, focusing on questions revolving around these three topics.

Alternatively, you can work through every topic for the exam, and then move onto past papers. The advantage of this method means that you can spend a chunk of time focusing completely on taking notes and using other revision techniques, then move onto working through whole mock papers. This means that you can simulate the experience of being in an actual exam.

Simulating Exam Conditions

Mock papers and past papers are really useful because they allow you to sit a test as if it was the real thing. To do this, find out how much time you would be given to finish the paper in an actual exam – this information can usually be found on the front of the past paper. Then, gather your pens, pencils and other tools, put your notes aside and find a quiet place. Then, get to work with the mock test.

Time yourself with a clock or stopwatch (most mobile phones come equipped with a stopwatch), and see how long it takes you to complete the paper. What's even more useful is to time how long each section, or even each question, takes you to complete. So, if you find yourself running short on time, you know exactly which topics or types of question need greater focus. You don't want to try and speed through your paper too quickly, but if you're taking an unusually long amount of time on shorter questions, then you know that you need to improve on them.

The best part of using mock exams and past papers is that you can put yourself to the test, and make sure of two things. Firstly, you can make sure that you can recall the material you'll need to remember in the real exam. This comes into effect when you simulate a real exam environment, by doing the test under timed conditions and without your notes. While you're doing the mock tests, you'll probably get an idea of what you can and can't recall. Whenever you can't remember the answer to a question, or there's a key fact you can't recall, make a note on a spare sheet of paper, or at the side of your answer booklet. Then, once you finish the paper, you know exactly what you need to go back to and revise some more.

Mock tests are also useful because they highlight things that you thought you knew, but perhaps didn't get entirely correct. This will become clear when you take a look at the mark scheme, which we will cover in more detail later on in this chapter.

After the Past Papers…

Once you're finished with the mock paper, look at the mark scheme and see how well you did. For subjects with clear "right or wrong" answers, such as Maths or the sciences, this is quite easy – all you need to do is read the answer then see if it matches what you wrote. For essay-based subjects such as English, this is trickier since the answers you give aren't necessarily right or wrong. In these exams, you tend to be judged on how well you write rather than what you write exactly. In this case, you might need help from your teacher.

Ask your teacher to take a look at your past papers, and they might be able to take a quick look at it. If they have the time, they might go ahead and mark it properly, giving you an idea of where you've done well and where you need to improve. If possible, get a full breakdown of marks so you know exactly what aspects of your exam you need to focus on.

In the next section, we'll examine a mark scheme in more detail. You'll learn how they work, and more importantly how to use them to make your revision more focused. For now, feast your eyes on the flowcharts. These show two different ways of including mock tests in your revision strategy.

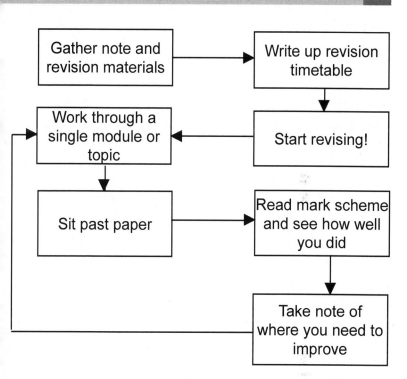

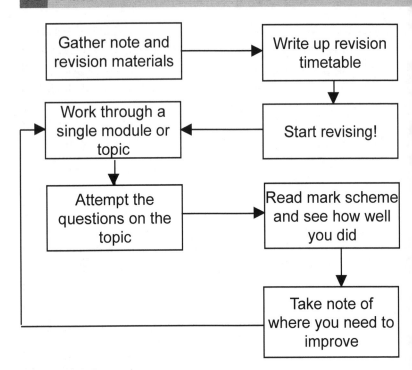

Mark Schemes

Once you've done some practice papers, you'll want to know how well you've done. As we've mentioned previously, mock papers show you what you need to remember, what you know and what you need to improve on. However, sitting the paper is only half of the story. You'll also need to use a mark scheme to figure out what you do and don't know.

What Are Mark Schemes?

Mark schemes are papers which examiners use when marking your exam. In the case of past papers, the mark schemes are the same ones which official A-Level examiners would use to mark your exams. So, they're the most accurate source for answers. Depending on the exam, a mark scheme will include different content. For example, Science exams will often simply give the correct answers since the questions are either right or wrong.

However, answers to essays in English papers aren't as straightforward. For exams with plenty of essay questions, the examiner will have criteria that they will need to look for in order to figure out what the quality of your work is. This is reflected in the mark scheme with a detailed description of what a higher-level essay will look like, and will compare it to other essays of all quality levels. This can make it difficult to mark your own essays, so having your teacher mark them is very useful.

Mark schemes and answer sections can usually be found in the same place where you downloaded the practice papers. Keep away from looking at the mark schemes until you've finished the papers – you don't want to spoil the tests – but have them ready to go.

What are the Benefits of Using Mark Schemes?

Exam Criteria – Essays

Mark schemes have uses beyond simply finding out whether you have the answers right or wrong. In fact, reading mark schemes can be useful even if you aren't sitting a past paper, because they'll show you what type of answers that the examiners are looking for. This is especially the case in essay-based exams, such as English, as well as other exams which include essays, such as Modern Foreign Languages, History and Geography. You can use mark schemes to find out what criteria the examiners use to mark your exams, and then compare what you've written to see how well you've done. Have you mentioned the key information that's listed for each answer? Have you answered the questions clearly, using an appropriate structure? Have you checked your spelling? All of these are going to be picked up on in essay-based exams, but it's worth reading a mark scheme to see how much each of these aspects affect your grade.

Jumping Through Hoops and Keywords

The other useful aspect of mark schemes is that they'll reveal key phrases and terms. A-Level is slightly different to GCSEs in this regard. At GCSE, you're often being tested on sheer knowledge and your ability to recall information. This means that knowing the key words is extremely important at GCSE level, and you can often net marks simply by dropping the key words into your answer.

However, this changes at A-Level. While knowing key terms is still important, in many subjects you're being assessed on *understanding* rather than regurgitation of key facts. This means that, while key terms are important, you want automatically earn marks just by mentioning them. Quite often, they have to have some kind of explanation, or application to a scenario. You'll need to engage your brain more for A-Levels.

With all this said, knowing what key terms tend to secure

the marks is important for succeeding in certain subjects at A-Level. You will need to remember key words in order to get better marks.

Exact Breakdown of Marks

Mark schemes can also be used to get an exact breakdown of an answer. Using the same example, the answer may award a single mark for lots of different things. For example, a question in a Biology paper could look like the following:

> *How does an asthma attack reduce airflow?*

One answer given could be:

> *When an asthma attack occurs, airflow is reduced because the following three things happen. Firstly, the muscle walls of the bronchioles tighten and contract, leading to a narrower space. Secondly, more mucus is produced by the bronchioles. Combined, this results in the diameter of the airways decreasing in size. This results in airflow being reduced.*

For this example, let's assume two things. Firstly, let's accept this as an entirely correct answer – it got full marks. Also, let's say that this answer is worth three marks. The mark scheme may distribute the marks as follows:

> *1 mark for mentioning each of the following:*
>
> • *Muscle walls of bronchioles contract/tighten;*
>
> • *The bronchioles produce more mucus;*
>
> • *Diameter of the airways are reduced.*

Now that we know what got us the marks, we can highlight them in the answer written.

> *When an asthma attack occurs, airflow is reduced because the following three things happen. Firstly, the <u>muscle walls of the bronchioles tighten and contract</u>, leading to a narrower space. Secondly, <u>more mucus is produced by the bronchioles</u>. Combined, this results in the <u>diameter of the airways decreasing in size</u>. This results in airflow being reduced.*

So, the breakdown of marks tells you exactly what you need to include in your answer, which will give you an idea of what you need to remember for the exam. Bear in mind that you might need to know more than what's given in the mark schemes, since you could be faced with a question which tackles the same topic but from a slightly different angle.

This information in the mark scheme means you could focus your answer even more. You might notice that a lot of the example answer is not underlined, and these details might not be necessary in order to gain full marks. With the information in the mark scheme, we can simplify and focus our answer:

Firstly, the <u>muscle walls of the bronchioles contract</u>. <u>More mucus is produced by the bronchioles</u>. Both of these <u>reduce the diameter of the airways</u>. This results in reduction in airflow.

Now this answer is much shorter, but should earn you the same amount of marks. So, we now have a much shorter answer, which will give us as many marks as the longer answer would. This saves time, allowing us to move onto other questions in the exam.

'Waffling' is what people tend to do when they aren't sure how to answer a question. Students who waffle in an exam will add lots of extra words to their answers to fill them out, even if none of what they are saying will earn them marks. We'll discuss waffling in more detail in the next chapter, but remember that reading a mark scheme and finding out exactly what earns you points should help you to avoid writing meaningless rubbish!

Giving Precise Answers

In an exam, you might be tempted to fire off everything you know about a topic all at once. While it's great that you've remembered lots of information, it's not always a good idea to write absolutely everything you know when answering a question. Instead, you should figure out exactly what the question is asking from you. In the above example, we included a lot of information that wasn't necessary to get full marks.

You should aim to be as precise as possible with your answer – get straight to the point in order to save time. Mark schemes are useful here, because they'll show you what the examiners are looking for. You can figure out what's required to get full marks in a question, then focus on giving that as your answer. In an exam, every second is precious; the less time you spend on unnecessary information, the more time you have for harder questions or for double-checking your work at the end. Efficiency is a great skill to have when it comes to exams, and using mark schemes to hone your answers will help you to achieve this.

As well as saving you time, working on giving precise answers can make you sound more confident when giving your answers. Too much information can come across as waffle.

With all this said, it's important that you make sure you answer every question in an exam as fully as possible. If you aren't sure what to write in your answer, it's better to give more information than less.

Examiners' Reports

The final pieces of documentation you can get from an exam board are called "examiners' reports". These are documents written by chief examiners at an exam board, drawing from exam results and mark breakdowns from previous years, to take note of what students as a whole did well, and where they need to improve. These can be useful for looking into larger questions, such as long essays, and finding out which areas students tend to fall down on. Then, you can compare this to how comfortable you are with the same elements, and in turn work a bit more on them if necessary. You can find these on exam board websites.

Conclusion

So, by this point you hopefully have the following: a revision timetable, a comfortable space to work, an idea of what your learning style is, and some ideas to get you started with revision. You've also been given some ideas about how to make use of both mock papers and mark schemes to increase your grade. You're now well on your way to taking your A-Levels and succeeding.

Next, we'll be looking at exams: what they are, how to deal with revising for them, and how to perform well in them!

Exam Techniques and Preparation

What Are Exams?

At this point in your academic career, you're probably quite familiar with exams. In fact, you're probably feeling too familiar with exams, and would especially like to get as far away from them as possible. Sadly, you aren't out of the woods yet, and you'll probably have to do at least one exam, but likely much more. In this section, we'll discuss how A-Level exams differ from those at GCSE.

As discussed in an earlier chapter, A-Levels expect more from you in multiple ways. When it comes to the exams, not only will the content be more demanding, but the questions themselves will probably expect you to do some problem-solving or critical analysis, depending on which subject you study. For example, English Literature at GCSE will focus on your ability to recognise themes and concepts in a text, but A-Level English Literature takes everything a step further – expecting you to critically assess these themes and concepts.

Unlike GCSEs, which are now all sat at the end of year 11, A-Levels are still split between AS levels (sat in year 12) and A2 levels (sat in year 13). This means that they'll be spread more evenly over two years, rather than forcing you to take all of them at the end of your final year. This should alleviate some stress.

It's also worth noting that A2 is usually worth more in terms of marks than AS. For example, the AS level may be worth 40% of your total A-Level, whilst A2 would be worth 60%. This may differ between subjects and exam boards, so check your exam board's website for a full breakdown of marks.

Finally, A-Level exams tend to be longer than GCSE papers. In recent years, GCSE papers have become longer, but A-Levels still tend to take more time to complete. In addition, questions are usually bigger and require more work to finish, but also have more marks available for each.

Grade Boundaries and Marks

Earlier in this book, we outlined the different grades available at A-Level, ranging from 'A*' to 'U'. This range of grades, as well as the grade you get, indicates the overall mark you got for a single exam, piece of coursework, or for a subject overall. For example, scoring 80% on an exam might give you an 'A', whilst 70% might be a 'B'. These numbers are known as grade boundaries – the minimum score required to achieve the associated grade.

The tricky thing about grade boundaries is that they aren't always set in stone, and the actual percentage required to achieve an 'A' might change every year, and will differ between subjects and exam boards. The reason for this is that grade boundaries are adjusted depending on the average grade scored by students in that year. In some cases, previous years of exam performance are taken into account as well. This means that, if the majority of students taking the exam score highly, then the grade boundaries will become stricter – to help differentiate between the high scoring students. For example, if the average mark in the exam is 10 marks higher than in previous years, students will generally require a higher mark to get a better grade. So, what might have been

70% for a 'B' in previous years, could be 75% in the current year.

The way this works is by converting your 'raw' mark (the mark you earned in the test) into what is known as a uniform mark scale mark (or 'UMS mark'). The difference between the two is that the raw mark is the actual mark on the paper. So, if the paper has a total of 80 marks available, there's 80 raw marks available. This can then be scaled up or down. One of the main reasons is to make it easier to make the numbers easier to work with. 80 in raw marks might end up being 100 in UMS marks. So, if you got 60 raw marks in the paper with a total of 80 marks, you'd get 75 UMS marks out of the total of 100. The boundaries are then applied to the UMS marks, and are shifted up or down in order to take factors into account, such as difficulty.

This has a couple of knock-on effects, which you need to be aware of. Firstly, it means that if the majority of students in the country find an exam incredibly difficult, then the grade boundaries could be more lenient to compensate for this. This also means that, if most students find an exam to be quite easy, the grade boundaries will be shifted to counteract it. The point of the grading system is to distinguish levels of ability and success, so it would make no sense for every student to get an 'E', and it wouldn't be helpful for everyone to get an 'A'. This means that if you revise everything well, and difficult questions still show up in the exam, don't panic! It's likely that everyone else feels the same way, and often this is taken into account by exam boards. Just answer the questions to the best of your ability.

Exam Tips and Techniques

Exams can be difficult, and you need to prepare for them in two different ways. First, you need to know the content of the exam. This is the actual information that you are going to be tested on – the stuff you've been learning in lessons.

The second thing you need to learn is how to answer exam questions, and how to perform well in exams. This might sound strange, but a significant part of doing well in exams comes down to your familiarity with them, not just how well you know your subjects.

In a later chapter, we'll discuss subject-specific tips for exams. For now, take a look at these general tips, which will help you in the days before and during your exams.

Practise Handwriting Beforehand

Since your exams are handwritten, you need to make sure that your handwriting is legible. In the exam room, people tend to write incredibly quickly. As the exam goes on, some students will write more frantically, while others might slowly ease into the exam and get better as time goes on. Either way, ensure that your handwriting is as easy to read as possible.

If the examiner can't read what you've written, they won't be able to mark your work. Generally speaking, it's only the most severe handwriting that results in a significant loss of marks, but if you know that your handwriting isn't as good as it could be, it's worth taking some time to practise it. If possible, try and incorporate handwriting practice into your revision so that you save time. Dedicated handwriting time is good, but you may as well kill two birds with one stone and use revision techniques that help your handwriting, such as making flashcards or writing out pages of notes. If you've been doing mock papers under timed conditions, this should have helped as well.

In the exam, make sure to take your time if you feel as though your handwriting is suffering. If it helps, ditch cursive (joined-up) handwriting so that the words are easier to read.

Finally, you want to practise handwriting so that your muscles are used to writing for extended periods of time. This is important for avoiding hand cramp. Find a way of gripping the pen which is as comfortable as possible, whilst also being able to write efficiently and neatly. Learning some exercises to gently warm up your hands before the exam can also be helpful, and will hopefully make you less worried about your hands giving up halfway through.

Come Prepared

Always make sure that you have all of the equipment necessary for completing an exam. This will depend on the subject and the module, so find out beforehand what you're allowed to take in with you.

The following are things that you can take into almost any exam:

• **Black pens.** You should always take a few black

ballpoint pens into your exams. Generally speaking, blue pens are not allowed, neither are fountain-pens, since the ink can run more easily on them. Ballpoints are the standard for most exam boards.

- **Pencils.** You might not need these for every exam, but it's worth bringing them for rough planning, just in case.

- **Clear pencil case.** Again, this might not be necessary, but bringing a pencil case can help you be more organised. Make sure it's clear though – if the exam invigilators can't see into the pencil case easily, they may confiscate it because you could be using it to hide notes and cheat!

- **Bottle of water.** We'll talk more about this later on, but bringing a bottle of water can help you concentrate – you don't want to get dehydrated. Remember to make sure that the bottle is clear and has no labels.

Depending on the exam, other pieces of equipment may be appropriate, such as:

- **Calculator.** Certain Maths and Science exams will allow you to bring calculators. Other exams in these subjects might not allow for calculators. If you aren't sure, bring it with you anyway and then leave it under your desk, and hand it to an invigilator if it isn't allowed.

- **Rulers and protractors.** Equipment for solving angles may be allowed for some exams. Like calculators, however, they won't be allowed for others. Make sure that they are transparent (clear).

- **Books.** Be careful with this one. Some exams might allow you to bring in a specific book, such as some English or language exams. Others will be referred to as 'closed-book' exams, which means you can't take in any notes or materials – including the books that you've studied.

If you aren't sure which equipment you're allowed to bring into the exam, ask your teacher well in advance.

Keep Calm

Getting a handle on your nerves can be really difficult during exam season, but remember that this is completely normal. If you consider that doing well in your A-Levels is very important, then it would be bizarre for you not to be at least a bit nervous. Millions of people will be going through the same thing as you, and millions more have been in your position and have made it out of the other end in one piece. Life goes on after your A-Levels, even if it doesn't feel like that during the heat of an exam.

Exams are stressful, and the conditions you take them in aren't pleasant either. Being stuck in a silent room for an hour, with nothing but a question paper and your own thoughts, can be incredibly daunting. However, you need to remember that you're not the only one who feels this way, and that a bit of nerves can give you the boost you need in the exam hall.

That said, you need to keep any anxiety under control. A breakdown just before the exam (or even worse, during it) is uncommon, but just remember that not doing as well as you'd hoped in a single exam isn't the end of the world.

You might feel as though you aren't prepared enough, or perhaps a classmate has made you unsure about what you've revised – minutes before entering the exam room. This happens often, and can be incredibly demoralising. Remember that how prepared you think you are doesn't necessarily represent how well prepared you actually are. Sometimes, people who feel poorly prepared for some exams in the minutes before taking it end up doing incredibly well, and some people find themselves doing worse in exams that they felt completely ready for. Essentially, you never truly know how prepared you are.

Besides, what's the use in worrying on the day of the exam? There's no time left to go back and revise some more, so there's no point in getting stressed about it once you're in the room. Try and get into the current moment and power through it.

If you're at AS level, remember that you've still got the next year to make up for things if you don't do as well as expected. A2 is usually worth more in terms of marks than AS level, so you can certainly make up for it the following year.

Here are some other tips for keeping calm in the exam:

• **Breathing exercises.** If you find yourself getting nervous before exams, or struggle to get to sleep due to exam anxiety, then breathing exercises could be beneficial.

- **Get into the moment.** Just before and during your exam, it can help to go into "exam-mode". By this, we mean blocking off outside distractions and any negativity coming from anywhere. Sometimes, having friends and classmates talk about the possible contents of the exam just before entering can put you off. It might make you feel as if you've missed out on something major, and then cause you to worry once you enter the exam room. Put all of this out of your mind as soon as you enter the room. Once you're in the exam, there's no use fretting about those details.

- **Positive thinking**. This might seem obvious, but thinking positively about the exam and what comes after can be extremely helpful. Some people like to change their mind-set about exams, thinking of it as an opportunity to show off their knowledge, rather than as a painful task that they have to work their way through. Alternatively, focus on what you **do** know rather than what you **don't** know, what you **can** do rather than what you **can't** do. Once you're in the exam room, there's no point worrying about your weaknesses. Focus on your strengths.

Read Instructions Carefully

This sounds simple, but far too many people trip up on this simple bit of advice. When you enter your exam, the first thing you should do is read the instructions on the front of the question or answer paper. In some cases, an invigilator may read the instructions to you, but feel free to read the instructions before the exam starts.

Keep an eye out for instructions on what questions to

answer. In some exams, you'll have a choice of which questions you answer, rather than having to answer every question. In these cases, you need to make sure that you know exactly what's required of you, so that you don't waste time answering questions that you don't need to answer. The only thing worse than finding out at the end of the exam that you answered questions unnecessarily, is realising that you didn't answer enough of them!

When you are given a choice of two or more questions to answer (especially in essay subjects), make sure you clearly show which questions you are answering. In some exams, you'll have to tick a box to show what question you're attempting, whilst others will require you to write the question number in your answer section. Either way, keep an eye on the instructions before going ahead and starting the question. This will prevent you from wasting time answering questions that you don't need to attempt, and also stop you from accidentally missing questions that need answering.

Answer the Easiest Questions First

This tip is absolutely key for the tougher exams you come across, since it's an excellent way to use your time in the exam hall effectively.

Say you're about to sit an exam. You sit down and have the examination instructions read out to you. The invigilator instructs you to start your exam, and then you begin. You open the question booklet to find that the first question seems almost impossible. Before you panic, take a flick through the booklet and take a look at some of the other questions. If possible, pick the question that looks the easiest to you and start with that.

This is a good technique for two reasons. Firstly, it's a great boost to your confidence when you're feeling unsure about the exam. There's not much worse in an exam than sitting there, becoming more and more demoralised by a question that you don't think you can answer. Starting with more manageable questions will help you ease into the exam, and hopefully you'll recall some information while doing it.

Sometimes, exams can fit together like a puzzle. At first, it seems impossible. But, once you start to put pieces in (answer the questions), the more difficult bits start to make sense. All of a sudden, you're on a roll of answering questions, and then the tough ones don't seem so bad!

The other reason that this is a good technique, is that it represents a good use of your time. There's no point sitting and staring blankly at a question that you can't solve, when there are others that you could be getting on with. Forget about the tough questions for now, bank as many marks you can get with the easier ones, then go back to the hard ones at the end if you have time. This way, you can secure as many marks as possible. In the worst-case scenario, you won't be able to complete the tough questions, but you'll still have earned a few points for all of the others.

Answer the Question

One of the biggest mistakes that students make throughout their academic lives is failing to answer the question that they've actually been asked. This is particularly the case for essay-based exams such as English Literature, but applies to all of your exams.

Focus on Key Details

Some students have a tendency to read a question briefly, then jump straight into their answer without thinking about what's really being asked. For questions which are worth lots of marks, you should take extra care in reading the question fully. If it helps, underline the key parts of the question, so that it's easier to break down:

> *What were the main causes of the First World War?*

This becomes:

> *What were the main causes of the First World War?*

We can figure out a few things from underlining the key points in this question. Firstly, we know that the topic of the question is the First World War. In particular, we need to be looking at the causes of the war. So, our answer is going to be focused on the time period leading up to the start of the First World War in 1914.

However, there's more to the question than this. This question specifies the "main" causes of the First World War. So, we don't need to talk about every single cause of the war, just a few of the most important or biggest things which caused the First World War to happen, such as the assassination of Archduke Franz Ferdinand and rising tensions between the European empires.

Already, we've figured out that we need to answer the

question in the following way:

- You need to talk about the causes of the First World War (events up to 1914).

- You need to limit your answer to the main (biggest) causes of the war.

Highlighting the key points of the question has proven useful, because it's pointed out exactly what the question is asking of us. This means that we can save time by answering exactly what we need to, rather than talking about things that won't get us any extra marks.

Don't Twist the Question

Sometimes, students see a question that they don't particularly like the look of. Perhaps it's for a topic that they've studied well and enjoyed, but the question takes a slightly different direction to one that they're used to. For example, a student may have studied the Shakespeare play *Othello* as part of English Literature, and really liked the dastardly villain, Iago. In the exam, they might come across a question on the play, but not specifically about Iago. The question could be:

> *How does Shakespeare show the relationship between Othello and his wife, Desdemona?*

This question is primarily focused on the main character, Othello, and his wife, Desdemona. While the character of Iago plays into most elements of *Othello*, it might be tricky to include him in a discussion about the relationship between Othello and Desdemona. So, you'd need to avoid straying from the topic of the question, even if there's something you would rather write about. Twisting the question into something that you want to answer is a trap that quite a lot of students fall into, and this ends up costing them marks – particularly in essay subjects. Writing a short plan for your answer, and reading the question carefully, can help you avoid this.

Double-Check the Question

In the next section, we'll be talking about double-checking answers, but it's just as important to double-check the question that you're answering, before you begin to answer it. Say you're doing a maths question:

$$8.93 \times 9.54 = ?$$

Before you start answering the question, take note of everything about it. Where are the decimal points? What operation needs to be performed? Sometimes, people make silly mistakes and misread the question, getting things mixed up.

It's not pleasant finding out that you've answered a question incorrectly just as you get to the end of it, so it pays to look over the question multiple times. In the case of maths questions, it might help to re-write the question in the answer box if there's space. This means you can look back at it quickly, without making any mistakes.

Don't Hedge Your Bets

Hedging your bets happens when a student tries to give 2 or more answers to a single question, trying to cover as many bases as possible and be less likely to lose marks.

After all, if you give lots of different answers, surely one of them is bound to be correct? The problem with this is that examiners will mark harshly against answers like these. Take a look at this example of someone who has tried to hedge their bets:

> *Question: What part of the human body carries blood back to the heart?*

> *Answer: Veins/Arteries*

Only one of the given answers can be correct, since one of them sends blood away from the heart and the other brings blood back to it. The correct answer is "veins", but in this example, both possible answers have been put in. This example answer shows that whoever answered the question wasn't sure, so put both down just in case. Examiners will not award marks for this, so it's essential that you don't try to play it safe in this way. Be confident in your answer.

Avoid Blanking

Have you ever been in a situation where you had something in your head that you were about to say, or about to write, but then completely forgot what it was just before saying or writing it? It can be frustrating in everyday life, but when it happens in an exam it can lead to all kinds of problems. Key details can be forgotten, formulas and tricks may be hard to recall, and sometimes you might just struggle to get off the first page. This is what people refer to as 'blanking'.

Blanking is something that many students worry about,

and you've likely heard some horror stories about people who have forgotten everything just as they enter the exam room. However, it doesn't occur as often as you might think, and it doesn't mean you're going to fail your exam.

The best way to prevent blanking is to keep stress to a minimum. This might be easier said than done, but students tend to blank when they haven't had much sleep or have tried to cram their revision into the day before, or the day of the exam itself. This can cause students to panic, and while they're busy worrying, anything that might have been holding in their short-term memory gets forgotten. We'll cover stress in more detail later in this chapter.

In addition to keeping stress to a minimum, make sure that you aren't revising on the day of your exam, and preferably not the night before, either. In order to retain the information in your revision, you need to commit it to what some people call your 'long-term memory'. It takes time for what you've studied to reach this part of your memory, and things revised in the hours before the exam usually haven't made it there. When revision is being held in the short-term memory, you're generally more likely to forget it, which in turn leads to blanking.

If you find that you've blanked in your exam, here are some tips to keep you calm and help you recover from it as quickly as possible:

Take a few deep breaths before continuing. This is important as you need to stay calm. The more you panic, the less likely you are to remember the information you need. Take a moment to calm down – remember that not performing so well on this exam isn't the end of the world, and that you have the entire paper to remember what you need to know and get back on form.

Look through the question booklet. Sometimes, the wording of a question can jog your memory, or give you a clue of what to write. This can get you started on an answer, which in turn can set off a chain-reaction of memories flooding back, to the point where you remember plenty of information. However, this doesn't always happen; don't rely on this as a replacement for revising over a longer period of time.

Start with an easier question. Some questions require less knowledge than others. If you find yourself blanking in the exam, go onto a question that doesn't need as much precise information as others. Sometimes, a question won't be asking for specific terms or details, but rather an analysis or critical take on the material. These are the questions to do first if you find yourself blanking. This won't work for every kind of exam, however.

Don't attempt any of the larger questions. It might be tempting to just throw caution to the wind and get the toughest or biggest question out of the way. This is usually a bad idea, since these questions contain the most marks. You want to answer these once you've remembered as much as possible, so wait until later in the exam to try them.

It's not the end of the world. If you find yourself running out of time, don't panic. Answer as many questions as you can to secure as many marks as possible. It isn't the end of the world if you don't do so well, and you'll have other exams in which to pick up some marks.

Double-Check Your Work

Everyone makes mistakes. It's almost completely unavoidable, even under relaxed conditions, to create a piece of work that's free of any errors at all. In an exam, you're going to feel a bit rushed, and you're probably going to be working very quickly. This is fine, but remember that you're more likely to make mistakes this way. So, it's important that you go back and check everything you've written. Small, silly errors can cost you big marks, so it's vital to make sure you've fixed anything that could be wrong.

Proofreading can take place at two times during your exam. You can either re-read each of your answers individually after you've completed each one, or you can go back at the end of the exam (if you have time) and check every question in one go. There are benefits and drawbacks to both:

Proofread as you go

Pros	Cons
You're more likely to have time to double-check your answers	If you spend too long proofreading, you might not finish the exam
You can take the exam bit by bit	You might be in "exam-mode" and not be as relaxed as at the end of the exam

Proofread at the end

Pros	Cons
You can focus on finishing the exam first before going back to check	If you take too long doing the exam, you might not have time to proofread towards the end
You'll probably be more relaxed once you've answered all the questions	

Both have pros and cons, and one method may just suit you better. You might prefer the methodical approach of checking every answer once you've finished it. Alternatively, you might find it easier to handle the exam, knowing that you've answered every question that you can, and then go back and check everything in one go.

How to go about proofreading your work will depend on the subject that you're taking, and the questions that you've been asked. If you've had to write essays or other longer bits of text, read over your work, checking for errors. Re-read the question, and make sure that you've answered properly. If you haven't done this, quickly add the extra information in the answer box.

If you've missed something out of an essay, the best thing to do is put a little asterisk symbol (*) where you'd like to add more information. Then, in the next available space (even at the end of the essay), put another asterisk, followed by the information that you've missed out on.

When you double-check your work, you might come across something that you've written, but that you know now is incorrect. In this case, you need to cross it out, so that the person marking your exam knows to ignore these incorrect parts. Put a straight, diagonal line through your work, to indicate any work that you don't want the examiner to look at. Then, all you need to do is replace what you've crossed out with something that's correct.

Bring Some Water and Eat Healthily

You are allowed to bring a bottle of water into almost any exam. There may be a couple of exceptions for practical-based exams – such as Art, but aside from that, water is allowed. In fact, bringing a bottle of water to drink in an exam is largely encouraged, because it can help you relax and concentrate.

Some studies show that students who take a bottle of water into their exams and drink it get an average score of 5% higher than students who do not. While this might not actually happen for you, this suggests that having a bottle of water handy can be helpful.

On the same topic, eating healthily (and sensibly!) before your exams can make a big difference. Try and avoid drinking fizzy drinks or eating sweets before an exam. The sugar rush might make you feel on top of the world when the exam starts, but you could have a crash halfway through, leaving you shattered for the final stretch. Instead, try and have a good breakfast in the morning before your exams. See what works best for you, but eggs and fish (such as smoked salmon) can give you plenty of energy to complete your exams with.

In addition to this, some exams may allow you to bring in a small piece of food to eat. Fruit is always a safe bet, including bananas and apples. Basically, you want something that doesn't take too long to eat, but gives you enough of a boost to help you through the exam. Remember to check that you're allowed to take food into your exam before doing so.

Stay Healthy

No matter what happens in your exams, it's important that you stay healthy. This is a slightly more general point, but it can't be emphasised enough.

First, you need to stay mentally healthy. Remember that there's life after your exams, and so you shouldn't put yourself under unnecessary pressure. Some anxiety is unavoidable, but it's important that you don't let it get out of control. Between exams, remember to do things that you enjoy, be it sports, video-games, reading fiction, watching television or spending time with friends or family. This will help you to feel calm during your exam period, and remind you that there's more to life than your A-Levels.

Secondly, you need to think about your physical wellbeing. While you're busy revising and making yourself ready to ace the exams, it's easy to forget about your own health. While it's good to take revision seriously, you can't neglect your own physical needs, and so you should make sure to get a lot of the following during your exam period:

- **Sleep.** Everyone needs sleep in order to function,

and you're no different! Teenagers and young adults need between 8 and 10 hours of sleep per night, so you should be aiming for this as well. A good night's sleep, particularly the night before your exam, can make a world of difference on the day of the test. It will also help you massively during your revision time.

• **A balanced diet.** This can be easily overlooked, but being fed well can be the key to acing an exam on the day. You want to feel as prepared as possible, so be sure to get a good meal the night before and on the day of your exam. Also, try to eat plenty of fruit and vegetables, since they help strengthen your immune system. Some students work themselves extremely hard, then forget to boost their immunity, leading to colds and flu. You want to avoid this – being ill during an exam is horrible!

Planning and Timing Your Exam

Good planning and timing are two of the most important skills that you can learn and practise before sitting your exams. In fact, being able to plan effectively and get your timing down will serve you well in almost every career, so it pays to put the effort in now.

Before you go into your exam, you should find out exactly what the structure of the exam will be.

Try and find out the answers to the following questions:

• How long do I have for the whole exam?

• What type of questions will be asked (essay,

single-word answer, short paragraph, problem solving, mathematical sums)?

- How many marks are there in the whole exam?

- Roughly, how many marks are available per question?

- If applicable, how much time is there for planning?

Once you have this information, you can get to work on applying this to your revision schedule. For example, when you attempt a mock exam, you should try to make the situation as close to the real thing as possible. You should plan and time your mock exam as if it were an actual exam. You can find more about planning and timing your exams in the chapter on subject-specific advice.

Stress

What is Stress?

Stress is an unpleasant sensation that you feel when you're under too much pressure. It's a common feeling to have as a student, especially when studying for and sitting your A-Level exams. The pressure that you feel can sometimes grow to become too much to deal with, and can be bad for your physical and mental health, as well as your A-Level performance.

Stress can be the result of several different worries about your A-Levels. Worries can include:

- Will I get the grades I want/need?

- Have I revised enough?

- Have I left it too late to start revising?

- What will my family and friends think of me if I don't do well?

- What if bad questions show up in my exam?

- What if I oversleep and miss my exam?

- What if I get into the exam hall and forget everything?

Rest assured that, no matter what you're worried about in the run-up to your exams, thousands of other students have felt similar things. It's quite normal to feel a bit stressed during the exam period. However, it's important to keep these pressures in check, and prevent stress from harming you or your chances of acing your A-Levels. The rest of this section will be devoted to discussing stress, and will hopefully give you some advice on how to manage and prevent it.

How Do I Know If I'm Feeling Exam Stress?

It can be difficult to know if you're stressed or not. Some people are genuinely stressed, but dismiss it as normal – perhaps because they do not know any different. If you're feeling stressed at all, it's important to identify it and make steps against it before stress becomes too much to handle.

The symptoms of stress occur because, when the body is under pressure, it releases hormones which trigger 'fight or flight' responses in the body. In prehistoric times, these symptoms may have proven useful for preparing the body to protect itself from a threat, or be able to run away quickly. Nowadays, we aren't particularly worried about fighting or escaping from wild animals, so the symptoms of stress aren't particularly helpful.

Stress has both emotional and physical symptoms. If you have any of the following symptoms, and feel unable to cope, then you might be stressed:

Emotional Symptoms	Physical Symptoms
Low self-esteem	Trouble sleeping
Anxiety	Sweating
Constant worrying	Loss of appetite
Short temper	Loss of concentration
	Headaches
	Dizziness

Whether you think you feel these symptoms or not, keep reading to find some methods for preventing stress, and some ways to reduce the stress that you may already have.

How Can I Prevent Exam Stress?

First of all, remember that exam stress is completely normal for students sitting their A-Levels. These exams are very important, and if you're feeling stressed about them it at least shows that you recognise their significance. While stress definitely isn't a good thing, the bright side of it is that you and your body are aware of how important your A-Levels are. Now what's needed is to keep your stress levels down so you can operate at peak performance, and more importantly stay healthy in body and mind!

This section will cover the "dos" and "don'ts" for dealing with exam stress, both during revision and the exams themselves.

DO...

Start revision early. This might seem obvious by now, but starting your revision earlier in the year is one of the best ways to avoid stress. The more time you have, the less you need to do each day. This gives you more free time, and also allows you to make use of extra time to do other revision activities such as practice papers.

Have a countdown to the end of your exams. Buy a calendar and make note of all your exam dates. Tick days off as they go by, and stay focused on the end. Staying aware of the end point of your exams will remind you that there's life after your A-Levels. There is light at the end of the tunnel.

Listen to your body. At times, you might feel like an unstoppable machine, speeding through revision. During this period, it can be tempting to ignore your bodily needs and soldier on. Likewise, when you're worried about not finishing your revision in time for the exam, it seems like a good idea to stay up all night to make up lost time. Whether you're ignoring your body because you're doing well or poorly, it isn't advisable to do so. You can't function properly without food, water and sleep, so remember to take the breaks in your revision to do these things. That way, when you come back to revising, your study sessions will be more valuable because you're able to focus harder.

Forget about the exam once it's over. It's likely that you'll have more than one exam. You might even have multiple exams on consecutive days, or even on the same day. So, it's important not to linger on an exam once you've finished it. As soon as the exam ends, you have permission to forget about it entirely. Try and avoid talking to others about details of the exam, because it might give you second thoughts about what you wrote in yours. There's no use worrying now since there's no way of changing what you've written. Stay confident and move onto the next exam.

Remember that exams aren't the be-all and end-all. As we've already mentioned, life won't end if you don't get top marks in an exam. You might be disappointed by your grade, but remember that life goes on and your exam results won't ruin your life. What's just as important is a confident and prepared attitude, so even if you don't do as well as you'd hoped to, you should focus on moving forward, learning from your mistakes, and enjoying life.

Ask others for support. No person is an island, and everyone occasionally needs someone else to help them through tough times. Exams can be difficult, and a lot of pressure is put on students taking their A-Levels. When the going gets tough, don't be afraid to talk to your friends and family. Find people you trust and talk to them about your worries. Sometimes, just talking about things can make you feel calmer, even if you don't figure out any solutions. More often than not, your worries will be amplified by the general worry of exams, and so talking through your problems and rationalising them can be a form of therapy. You might find that your worries are just the result of paranoia, and aren't grounded in reality.

DON'T...

Rely on online forums. The internet can be an excellent place to find information and techniques for studying. You have access to plenty of specific advice on a range of subjects, and this can supplement your work in the classroom and your revision at home. However, not all resources are useful, and not all environments on the internet are good for your wellbeing. Some exam-focused chatrooms and forums can do more harm than good. You may come across people who are arrogant about the work that they've done, trying to make you feel worse about your studies as a result. Make use of the internet when it comes to your A-Levels, but try not to linger in places that won't make you feel better about your own studies.

Pay attention to how much revision others are doing. You'll likely find classmates who are all too willing to let you know how much revision they're doing, and how well their revision is going. These people are probably having a really hard time with their revision, and are just looking for a way to feel better about themselves. If you need to, ignore these people until your exams are over, and instead spend your free time with people who don't stress you out as much.

Get lazy because your friend has done less revision than you. Just as you'll probably come across someone who's apparently done a lot of revision, you probably have a friend or classmate who has apparently done no revision at all, or very little. While they might be telling the truth, it's also possible that they've actually done quite a lot of revision and they claim to have done little in order to look cool. It's tempting to get lazy about your revision because there's someone else who's done less, but remember that exams aren't about how well others are doing: it's about how well **you** are doing. In turn, this could lead to stress as you realise that you haven't done enough just before the exam. Make sure that you avoid getting lazy with your revision, and this will be far less likely to happen.

Set goals you can't meet. Always remember that there's only so much that you can do each day when it comes to revision. If you've put together a revision timetable then this shouldn't be a problem, but double-check how much work you've allotted for each day. During the revision period, take note of how much you're doing each day, and adjust your timetable based on this. For example, if you're finding that 10 topics is far too many, try reducing it to 7 or 8. Likewise, if you're able to do loads more than 5, experiment and see how many topics you get through in one day. The aim of this is to finish each day satisfied that you did everything you can, and that everything is completed. This should work towards preventing exam stress.

Panic about your exam timetable. Occasionally, you might not meet all of your goals for the day. While this isn't a good thing, you need to remember that you always have the next day to cover what you failed to achieve the day before. At the end of your revision for the day, you should try and put yourself in the mind-set that everything is fine – meaning that you can relax and get some quality sleep.

Rely on caffeine or other stimulants. Caffeine will affect your concentration and sleep-patterns. If you become dependent on it, you'll find yourself unable to perform properly without it, which could lead to uncomfortable and unproductive revision sessions. This could cause stress over time, as you require a certain chemical in your body in order to feel ready to study or sit an exam. In addition, interrupting your sleeping-pattern can make you feel tired during your study time, and can cause stress in general. Do yourself a favour and keep away from the caffeine during the exam period.

Advice for Parents

Stress is felt amongst most students sitting their GCSEs and A-Levels. While it's normal to be slightly anxious about exams, you should keep an eye on how your son or daughter is behaving. As a teenager, they may be quite defensive or quiet about their feelings towards exams, but if you see any of the symptoms listed earlier in this section, you should consider helping them. Here are a few of the ways in which you can help your son or daughter avoid feeling stressed during their exam period:

• **Make sure that they know you're happy to talk with them about their worries.** You don't need to pester them, but if you notice that they're stressed, reminding them that they can talk to you whenever might convince them to open up a bit and talk. This could help them relieve lots of built-up stress.

- **Set time aside to talk to them if necessary.** Don't just let your son or daughter know that you're there to talk to, make sure that you're available at relatively short notice. This might not be possible during your own working hours, but while you're not at work, be ready to stop what you're doing and chat with them. They'll really appreciate you being able to talk whenever they need you.

- **Respect their free time.** Teenagers hate being nagged to do things, especially revision. You need to make sure that they're actually working, but you also need to respect their free time and not interrupt them. One way to fix this is to ask for a copy of your son or daughter's revision timetable, so that you know when they should be working and when they will be taking a break. This means that you know not to disrupt their breaks or free time by asking them whether they should be working or not. They'll likely appreciate this, since it allows them to relax after a hard day of revision.

- **Give them what they need to succeed.** Make sure your son or daughter has good food, to help them study and prevent stress. Ask them if there's anything in particular that they feel is necessary in order for them to do well, and help them in any way you can.

Conclusion

As you probably already know from sitting your GCSEs, exams can be incredibly difficult. Sadly, A-Levels are no exception, and in fact they might be the toughest exams you'll take in your life. With all that said, remember that the purpose of A-Levels isn't to catch you out, or cause you to fail. A-Level is an environment designed to gauge your ability, and if you've followed the advice given up to this point in our guide, you're well on your way to unlocking your full potential.

Also, bear in mind that you're not the first person to take A-Levels, and you probably won't be the last either. This means that there have been years of perfecting A-Level courses and exams, so you shouldn't be worried about anything unfair coming to the surface while you're completing them.

If there's absolutely one thing that you must take away from this, it's that exams aren't the be-all and end-all in your life. They're certainly important, and you should take them seriously, but don't let yourself become distraught over worries about exams, or results which weren't as high as you might have hoped. There's much more to life than your A-Levels.

In the next chapter, we'll be discussing the ins and outs of coursework.

Coursework and Controlled Assessment

Depending on when you sat your GCSEs, you may or not be familiar with coursework. In recent years, coursework has been phased out of the GCSE curriculum, meaning that you might not have done it before beginning your A-levels. However, coursework is still very relevant to students at A-Level, particularly for those studying essay-based subjects such as History and English Literature. In addition, a lot of technology and art subjects still expect students to finish some kind of project. In this chapter, we'll be covering what coursework is, what's generally expected of you, and how to come out of it with a grade you can be proud of.

What is Coursework?

Coursework (or 'controlled assessment') is a method of assessment used by exam boards and schools to test students. Unlike exams, in which the actual assessment takes place in an exam room for a few hours, coursework is assessed over a much larger period of time. Depending on your subject and exam board, this could differ slightly. As of 2017, there are three ways in which your coursework assessment can be structured:

- 'Informal' coursework – this is when students complete their coursework over a longer period of time and then hand it in on the deadline;

- 'Formal' controlled assessment – this is when students prepare over a period of time, then write their coursework submission under timed, pseudo-exam conditions;

- A hybrid of the two – this occurs when students

complete their coursework over a longer period of time, but each session is monitored in some way.

The kind of course structure will depend on your subject, specification and exam board. To find out more about whether your subject contains coursework, and how that coursework is organised, ask your teacher or check your exam board's website. Whatever the case, you'll likely find that coursework gets started (and finishes) a considerable amount of time before exam season starts. This means you don't need to worry about coursework by the time you get to your exams.

Coursework tends to be marked by either your teacher or another teacher in your school, and is then moderated by an external examiner representing your exam board. These moderators are brought in to ensure that teachers are marking the coursework fairly. Depending on the number of coursework submissions in your school, the moderator may check some of the papers, or even all of them.

Coursework tends to be worth a significant part of your overall A-Level grade for a single subject. Often, they're worth somewhere around 20%, but some can be much higher. 20% is the difference between an 'A' and a 'C', so it's vital that you take it seriously. In this chapter, we'll cover some tips on how to ensure that your coursework reflects your ability as much as possible.

Extended Project

As well as coursework for specific subjects, extended projects are often available for students at A-Level.

Students usually take these as one of their A-Level subjects, but some will take them alongside their three or four A-Levels.

Extended projects can manifest in a number of ways. Many students tend to do a written report, which involves research in order to complete. In other cases, students may wish to do a production, such as a sports event or a fashion show. The final option for an extended project is an artefact, which constitutes pieces of art or products such as video games or some other kind of design which has been planned and then created.

It's clear that extended projects are incredibly open-ended, and students will be expected to do all of the following:

- Choose a topic;

- Choose a medium (written project, production, or artefact);

- Plan the project;

- Conduct research on the project;

- Develop their idea into a finished product.

So, an example of someone's project could be the following:

Topic	Short film about the pressures of studying A-Levels
Medium	Artefact (a film)

From here, the student would need to plan a number of things. Firstly, they'd need to plan their time. Someone studying an extended project like this would need to consider the following:

- How much time is going to be spent researching the project?

- How long is needed to write the script?

- What equipment (lighting, cameras, editing software) will I need? What props will I need, and where will I get them?

- Do I need to find willing actors to participate?

- How long will it take to film everything?

- How long will it take to edit it?

- Am I proficient in writing, filming and editing?

All of these, and more, will need to be considered before starting the extended project. Of course, the amount of planning required will differ depending on your topic and medium. Nevertheless, extended projects require a lot of work, and must be taken seriously. Since they're similar to coursework in terms of its structure and the length of time required to complete it, the advice in this chapter will be useful for those undertaking an extended project.

Tips for Acing Your Coursework

Start as Soon as Possible

Many students make the mistake of putting coursework

off because they think the deadline is far off in the distance. You might not need to write up the final piece until months away, so why bother doing any work now? This is an easy trap to fall into, but must be avoided to perform well. Find out from your teacher as soon as possible what the topic of your coursework is, and what suitable work you can do. In some cases, this might be reading or research, whilst in other scenarios it could be simply becoming familiar with the material. Whatever the case, try to get started as soon as you can – it'll pay off as you approach the deadline.

Get a Structure and Stick To It

When your coursework takes place over weeks or months, it's easy for it to get out of control and lose any sense of coherence. What you end up with when you reach the deadline might be completely different to what you intended it to be. This isn't always a bad thing, but having a plan for your coursework as soon as possible is a good idea, because it means that you have more control over what you're making.

There are two different things to consider when starting a piece of coursework:

- How to plan your time;

- How to plan your work.

Getting together a plan of how you're going to use your time when completing your coursework is key to making sure you meet the deadline with everything finished. You don't need to keep a completely strict schedule,

but having structure will keep you working a
coursework from piling up. In this example, let's sa
you have a controlled assessment in History. You kr
that you'll have to write all your work in a few sitting
and in a controlled environment, essentially under exam
conditions. However, up until that point you'll need to be
doing research, taking notes, planning your essays and
possibly writing up drafts, just so you can get an idea of
what you're going to write in the real thing.

Since most controlled assessments are completed
earlier in the year (before the revision starts), you're able
to devote plenty of time to your coursework. Here's an
example plan over 8 weeks, leading up to the deadline.
For each week, there are a few objectives to meet,
followed by some other considerations relevant to the
task.

	...uestion(s) or topic(s) (if there's
	Which questions seem most interesting?
	Start a mind map of ideas, considering the following:
	• What is the question asking?
	• What general areas do I need to research?
Week 2	Begin research on the topic:
	• What sources are available?
	• Do I need to find additional sources?
	• How many sources do I need to include?
	Construct a timeline of events which relates to the topic you're writing about.
Week 3	Start making notes based on research. Remember to include where you got your ideas from. Try to get a mixture of statistics and other facts.

Week 4	Construct a rough essay plan:
	• What's the word limit for the controlled assessment?
	• How many points do I need to cover?
	• What is the argument I want to make?
Week 5	Make your plan more detailed by applying the notes you've made to your rough plan:
	• Try and have plenty of evidence for each point you're going to make.
	• Make note of which evidence you've already used for a point so that you don't re-use the same content.
	• Write a rough conclusion for your essays, so that you have a good idea what the end point of your work is.
Week 6	Try writing some of your points as full sentences rather than rough notes, then have a go at linking your points together in full paragraphs.
Week 7	Try writing a full essay based on your plan. You can use this to get some practice in typing up a piece of work in a short space of time.
Week 8	Final week – write the coursework in a controlled environment.

This is a rough plan for a single subject. Of course, the type of work you'll be doing will depend on what the subject is, and therefore what's appropriate in a plan will change. However, the table above should give you an idea of how to complete an extended piece of work before jumping into it.

Remember that some subjects prevent you from taking coursework home, in order to prevent students from cheating or tampering with their own work. Consult your teacher before taking any work home. If your teacher has constructed a week-by-week plan, try making use of theirs before creating your own.

Make Use of Multiple Drafts

If you are doing a long-term piece of coursework that allows for the teacher to read and mark your work, make use of it. Some students will simply work on their draft, finish it and then forget about their coursework until the deadline, when they hand in the exact same piece of work. Multiple drafts are there to help you refine your work, so make use of them as much as possible.

Listen to Feedback

If you get the opportunity to have your drafts read by a teacher, listen and take on board what they suggest you improve on. Sometimes it can be difficult to look at criticism of your work, but it's essential if you want to make your coursework better. Bear in mind that your teacher is there to help you, not attack your work or embarrass you.

Don't Try and Finish It in One Sitting

Some students try to complete all of their coursework in

one go – usually the night before the deadline. This is never a good idea, and often results in rushed work full of errors. Earlier in this chapter, we provided an example week-by-week plan of how to bring a piece of coursework to completion. Create one of these for yourself and follow it to make sure that you aren't suddenly faced with a mountain of work the night before the deadline.

Proofread

Proofreading has been talked about in the exam techniques section, but it's just as important when completing coursework. Double check everything you've written or made. If possible, compare it to a mark scheme, to ensure that you have met all of the requirements to get the grade that you want.

Depending on what kind of coursework you're doing, you're going to want to look out for different things. Of course, checking spelling, punctuation and grammar is important for any piece of work, but you also need to make sure that the content is sound as well. If you've included statistics or other facts in your work, go and compare what you've written to the place you found the information. Do the numbers all add up? Are the facts correct? Make sure that what you've presented is as accurate as possible before submission.

Avoid Plagiarism

Plagiarism is the act of reproducing somebody else's work without their permission, and is taken very seriously by both schools and exam boards – especially when it comes to coursework. It isn't so much of a concern in exams, since copying someone else's work is difficult and doesn't happen often, but in coursework there are lots of regulations to make sure that students hand in work that is their own. This could be one of the reasons why coursework has moved from a less-restricted, open task, to something more structured and controlled, with students finishing their controlled assessment in a classroom while being supervised.

Whatever the case, avoiding plagiarism is vital when completing coursework. Not only is it against regulations and can result in your work being disqualified, but it's also unfair on the people who have worked hard to create the material that you might be copying. Whether it's your classmate, a website, or a book, you should never copy someone else's work.

Conclusion

As previously mentioned, coursework is becoming less relevant every year, and it's entirely possible that you haven't had to complete any at all, depending on your subject choices. If you do have coursework, think of it less as an obstacle or a chore, and more of an opportunity to score marks before entering your exams. The better you do in your coursework, the more secure your overall grade will be if the exams don't go quite as well as planned.

In the next chapter, we'll cover subject-specific advice for a number of the most popular subjects studied at A-Level.

Subject-specific Revision Advice

So far, we've given you lots of general advice for revision, exam performance and coursework achievement. While these tips will apply to pretty much every subject available at A-Level, there's more to be said about individual subjects. In this chapter, we'll be taking a look at the most popular subjects at A-Level. Our aim is to show the following:

1. What these subjects are composed of in terms of exam and coursework content;

2. The layout and structure of exam papers and coursework;

3. Revision techniques which work especially well for each subject;

4. What you're being tested on for each subject.

We'll be going into as much detail as possible, but bear in mind that the syllabus for each subject will differ to some extent based on the year it's being studied, the exam board the course is on and the specific course. Beyond that, schools have some autonomy when it comes to certain subjects. For example, schools are usually able to choose the material studied in English Literature – particularly for the coursework side. This means that the examples given in this chapter won't necessarily suit what you're studying. However, the examples aren't what's important – it's the advice they demonstrate that you need to take on board and make use of!

We'll be going into detail on the following subjects:

- Maths;

- English Literature;

- Sciences (Biology, Chemistry, Physics);

- Languages;

- History;

- Geography;

- Social Sciences (Psychology, Sociology).

You might notice that there's some crossover between these tips. For example, advice for the English Literature exam about critical analysis will be useful for History. Likewise, some of the methodology for remembering formulae for Maths could be applied to any other subject which requires some mathematical problem-solving, such as the sciences. Also, don't panic if your favourite subjects aren't mentioned specifically in this chapter. Some of these tips will be useful to you regardless of the subjects that you're taking.

Maths

Maths at A-Level is entirely exam-based, and is made up of a number of modules which cover the following fields:

- Core mathematics;

- Statistics;

- Mechanics;

- Decision mathematics.

As of 2017, all Maths students need to take four modules of core mathematics (C1, C2, C3 and C4), as well as three more modules in any of the remaining areas. Alongside their four core mathematics modules, students will need to study either mechanics, statistics, decision mathematics, or some combination of the three. Here are the modules available at A-Level maths:

Mechanics	Statistics	Decision	Core
M1	S1	D1	**C1**
M2	S2	D2	**C2**
M3	S3		**C3**
M4	S4		**C4**
M5			

*(Modules marked in **bold** are mandatory.)*

Generally speaking, you must complete earlier modules in a subject before being able to take later ones. That means you can't jump straight into M5 for mechanics – you'd need to study M1 to M4 first. This is the case because Maths tends to be a cumulative subject – skills you learn earlier on will help you in later modules. So, if you want to go all the way to M5, you'll need to study M1-M4. The only way to do this is to study Further Mathematics, which we'll talk about a bit later in this chapter. Students taking regular Maths A-Level will have to do six modules in total.

As you can imagine, each subject within the overall Maths A-Level course covers different areas of mathematics. Here are some of the topics you can expect to find in each of the subjects:

Core Mathematics (C1, C2, C3, C4)	Algebra, functions, coordinates, differentiation, integration, trigonometry, exponentials, and logarithms.
Mechanics (M1, M2, M3, M4, M5)	Vectors, kinematics, centres of mass, dynamics, collisions, motion, and stability.
Statistics (S1, S2, S3, S4)	Probability, correlation, regression, distribution and estimation.
Decision (D1, D2)	Algorithms, linear programming, allocation, game theory and dynamic programming.

Over the course of your Maths A-Level, you'll likely come across other topics as well. The exact specification will also differ depending on your exam board and the year you sit the exam. Make sure to check your exam board's website to find out exactly what you'll be studying in each module.

Further Mathematics

Students who find that they have a particular aptitude for mathematics might find themselves wanting to take Further Maths. This is an extension of the Maths course which acts as a full A-Level. So, you could finish your A-Levels with an A-Level in Further Maths as well as Maths.

Students studying Further Maths will have to take more modules than those sitting regular Maths A-Level. As well as the six modules taken for Maths, Further Maths students will have to take another six modules, including three further pure maths modules (FP1, FP2, and FP3). From here, you need to take three modules from the list above. This means that the later modules (i.e. M4, M5, S4) will be available to you.

Tips for Maths Revision

At A-Level, Maths is all about learning rules and methods, and then applying them to problem-solving scenarios. For this reason, the only way to get better at Maths is to practice doing questions, either from past papers or textbooks. However, you can use the following breakdown to structure your Maths revision:

Make a note of everything you need to learn. As previously mentioned, you can find every topic you'll need to know for each module in the course specifications. You might need to download these from your exam board's website, but your teacher may also have a list of every topic that you need to learn. Either way, take every topic, formula, and rule, then sort them into a checklist. Try to keep them in the same order that they're taught, since your ability to understand some units will depend on how much you know about earlier topics. Use this checklist as a guide to your Maths revision, and tick topics off once you've finished them.

Learn your rules and formulae. Think of these as tools required to solve questions. You need to make sure that these are ingrained in your long-term memory so that you can call upon them at any time. Visual learners can benefit from writing out the rule or formula, folding the sheet of paper over so it's concealed, then trying to write it again from memory. Keep doing this until you feel confident that you can remember the rule or formula easily. Test that you can do it at least ten times, before moving onto the next one.

Attempt some questions. You might need your notes handy to begin with, but you should focus on correctly answering questions using your memory. Take your time answering these questions – your goal is to make sure that you understand the material at every step. If you get stuck on a particular area, check your notes and then try to complete it with them to hand. If you still find yourself unable to continue with a question, make a note of it and speak to a classmate or your teacher about it, and see if they can shed some light on where you're going wrong.

Preferably, you should aim to be capable of completing ten questions of a specific type, without referring to your notes, before moving onto the next topic or question type.

Attempt practice papers. Once you're confident in your ability to solve questions without referring to your notes, you're probably ready to take a look at practice papers. Start by familiarising yourself with the layout of the paper, but swiftly move on to completing the paper under exam conditions. In the next section, you can get some advice on how to perform well in the exam, which will also apply to doing well in the mock papers.

In the Exam…

As with most A-Level subjects, exams will be split across 2 years. This means that, in your first year of A-Levels, you only need to revise for the exams you'll be sitting at the end of the year. This makes things a little easier on yourself.

Depending on your exam board, the length of exams will differ. Some specifications have 90-minute-long exams, whilst others are 2 hours long. The number of exams you'll have to sit will differ depending on your exam board and specification as well. Check your exam board websites before structuring your revision timetables, so you know exactly what you're getting into.

In the exams, you're essentially being tested on your ability to recall formulae, rules and techniques in order to solve mathematical problems. Like GCSE, the more demanding questions start to appear towards the end of the paper, although this rule isn't followed so strictly. What's also similar to GCSE is that the more demanding questions are worth more marks, so it's important that you attempt them during your exam.

Make sure that you include working for all of your answers, clearly labelling each step as you go. A good rule for keeping your flow of mathematical deduction clear is to devote a whole line to each step, and then number each line, so that the examiner can distinguish between them. Then, if you need to refer to a specific line in your working, you can simply include the number of that line in brackets. Remember that this isn't a method for saving time, and your answers should be written out fully and clearly, but being able to refer to a specific line may be useful when showing your answer at the end of your attempt. It also helps you keep track of what is on each line, making it easier for you to double-check your work.

Speaking of double-checking, taking a look back over your answer is a great way of making sure that you've answered the question correctly. Before you even start the question, you should read it carefully, making sure that you understand the instructions given to you. Additionally, make sure you don't misread the content of the question. People get stressed under exam conditions, making it more likely to not follow the question properly, which can result in disaster. Double-check the question before you even start it.

Once you've finished a question, make sure you've answered it correctly. Even if you thought the question went well or was quite easy, it's entirely possible that you've slipped up at some point. This doesn't mean that you're incompetent or sloppy in your skills; everyone makes mistakes, you just need to make sure that they don't cost you marks.

Finally, make sure that you clearly mark which question you are attempting before you begin to answer it. Put the number and letter of the question on the left-hand-side of the answer area (e.g. 1a, 3b, 7c) so that your examiner knows what work corresponds with each question.

English Literature

A-Level English Literature incorporates exams and coursework into its assessment scheme. Generally speaking, exams are found at AS and A2 level, but coursework is usually reserved for A2. However, this may differ depending on the exam board. What also differs between exam boards is how much the coursework is worth. It's usually worth around 20% of your A2 level, which is quite a significant amount. In this section, we're going to focus on preparing for English Literature exams, but our tips regarding critical analysis remains useful for coursework.

Like GCSE, A-Level English Literature looks for a strong grasp of the material that you've studied, be it poetry, a Shakespeare play, or a 20th Century novel. You'll need to know the main themes of each work that you've studied, as well as how these themes link and crossover. English at A-Level is less about jumping through hoops and writing the "right thing" that the examiner wants to see, but it is more about articulating a response to questions which shows individual thought and a wider understanding of literary criticism.

You might be wondering "how can I come up with a unique response?" The answer to this is complicated for a number of reasons. Firstly, you'd be right to believe that you can't come up with a completely unique answer. The way you think of a text will be influenced by the ideas of others, and the ocean of interpretation and critique of the books, plays and poems that you're studying will probably have already come up with what you want to write. In that sense, creating a completely unique idea isn't possible. The examiners are aware of this, and won't necessarily mark you negatively for acknowledging interpretations that others have made.

You also need to remember that you aren't expected to make great, sweeping statements about the text you're studying. You probably only have an hour to plan and write your answer, so no examiner is expecting you to have a revelation and create a sea-change in critique of *Macbeth.* For this reason, don't try to be grandiose in your argument – tighten your focus exactly to what the question is asking, and then work within those parameters to get a response.

So, to summarise this information on creativity, you should try to **avoid** the following:

1. Creating a completely new interpretation of the text which completely ignores current criticism;

2. Making grandiose, sweeping arguments about the text in an attempt to create a completely new idea.

The best way to avoid both of these points is to create a nuanced argument. By this, we mean that you need to focus on specific areas, and try to create small (yet interesting) observations and criticisms of the work. Your entire essay might focus on just a few lines of dialogue, supplementing it occasionally with other ideas and material in the text. Focusing your view onto something specific will make it more likely that you can flesh out an interesting argument in the time given. Remember: you don't have months to write a companion book to your favourite Shakespeare play – you have maybe an hour at most to construct your argument. Your examiner is well aware of this, so be confident in creating a focused, nuanced argument rather than a sprawling, messier one.

You also want to refer to wider criticism where appropriate. You don't have to do this often, but demonstrating that you've read more widely than the text will earn you more marks in the exam, especially if you implement them well. You can't just shoehorn unrelated ideas from other writers into your essay, so you'll need to get hold of a range of different interpretations in order to prepare for any kind of question.

Another important area to consider for A-Level English is how well you address context. Knowledge of society at the time the text was written will enhance your mark significantly. For example, if you're aware of how male-centric society in the mid-19th Century was, then Cathy's role in *Wuthering Heights* can be critiqued more eloquently. On the one hand, she's one of the central characters, but at the same time she's completely helpless – conveying the low status of women at the time. There's more to it than that, but this should give you an idea of how to incorporate context into your argument. Again, you need to stay relevant – you can't throw in any old facts about the time period, you need to make sure they support your argument!

Between references to wider reading and acknowledgement of context, you're well on your way to proving that you've thought carefully about the text. Ultimately, you need to construct an argument that's well-supported by the text, and if you do these things *and* insert some personal style, you're bound to score highly.

Tips for English Literature Revision

Revising for an English exam is strange because you aren't being assessed purely on what you know. In Maths or the sciences, you're going to be giving 'right or wrong' answers, and getting the answer right will depend on how much you know. For example, if you don't know how to perform differentiation, you aren't going to be able to complete the questions which involve it. For these subjects, knowledge is a strict barrier for entry. This is even the case in other 'essay-based' subjects such as History, where knowing facts and statistics is vital, with some interpretations of historical events being preferable to others (or, at the very least, easier to argue for).

The relationship between knowledge and success in English Literature is slightly different. While you're being judged on how well you argue rather than exactly what you've written, you need some knowledge in order to perform well. Some people manage to bluff their way through some English papers, but those who come prepared are much more likely to do better. In this section, we're going to take a look at what you need to know, and how you can make sure you've remembered it.

Read the material. This might sound obvious, but quite a lot of students don't bother to read the text outside of the classroom, instead relying on online synopses and second-hand notes. While these are both incredibly useful, they should be used to supplement your reading, rather than replacing it. Reading the material is an important starting point for your revision. While it might not feel like a good use of time, there's a level of insight that you get from reading a text that you won't get from reading a synopsis.

For example, you could easily look up the most important quotes from *Othello* and use them in your exam, but if you do this then your answer will look just like everyone else's. Of course, these quotes are considered important for a reason – they often demonstrate key themes and concepts – so you should make use of them. However, it doesn't hurt to have some lesser-known quotations up your sleeve to make your argument more nuanced.

Underline or make note of the key quotes. In an English exam, quotes are your tool for making and supporting your argument. You can't really make a claim about a text if there's no hint of it in the content, form or structure! For this reason, getting a collection of quotes saved in your mind is key to performing well at A-Level.

Once you've finished reading the text(s), it's time to head back in and start making note of anything that may be useful to you in the exam. In particular, think about the key themes of the text and find parts of the text which relate to them. For example, if fate is a key theme of *Romeo and Juliet*, you'll want to make note in reference to "star-cross'd lovers". This is the stage where you can use workbooks and online resources to supplement your learning, since they'll likely have a list of key quotes that you can refer to. Combine this with some quotes that you've chosen, and you'll have a wealth of resources to help you form an argument.

Organise quotes into themes. Sadly, there's no way of telling what the exact topic of the exam questions will be. You may be asked to contrast between multiple texts, explore characters and/or themes, and more. Although you don't know exactly what you'll be up against, you can probably figure out a list of themes – one or more of which will appear in your exam. For example, if you happen to be studying an anthology of First World War poems, you might categorise your quotes into the following themes:

Patriotism	Nature	Humanity	Death
Love	Decay	Hopelessness/ futility	Cruelty
Separation	Exhaustion	Government/ politics	

Organising your quotes like this means that you can compartmentalise them better in your mind. It also allows you to create links to quotes within the themes, and even with other themes as well.

Revise your quotes. Once you've got everything together, it's time to make sure you remember all of the quotes you'll need. Depending on what kind of learner you are, the best way to do this will differ. Visual learners may find that writing the quotes down, covering the paper and writing it again and again from memory helps them stick in your mind. Flashcards can be used here as well – the key theme can be written on one side of the card, and the quote itself could be on the other. Aural learners could record themselves saying the quotes out loud, then listen back to them in order to keep them in their head. Find methods which work for you and revise them until you can comfortably recite or write the quotes down.

Find wider reading to supplement your quotes. Once you've got a robust collection of quotes from the main text, you'll want to find other material to support it or contrast with it. This will differ depending on your exam board, but some English exams expect use of wider reading to enhance an argument. In fact, exams with this requirement tend to set aside marks for the use of wider reading. In these tests, you need to show that you've read more than just the main text.

Wider reading can come in two forms. Firstly, there's wider reading in the form of other novels, plays and poems that you can use to compare characters or themes. For example, you might want to examine how two different texts convey the theme of unrequited love. This is where your wider reading will come in useful. You can organise these into themes in the same way you did for the main text's quotes.

Read up on context. This won't take nearly as much time as revising quotes, but taking note of the context for each of the texts you'll be writing about in the exam can be incredibly helpful. This works as a supplement to the rest of your answer, and where appropriate acts as a kind of garnish to your essay. Make sure you have a few bullet-points about the following:

- The society the creator of the work (author, poet, playwright etc.) lived in;

- The background of the creator (gender, class, etc.);

- Key events surrounding the writing of the work, such as lost lovers, family deaths, or involvement in wars;

- How all of the above may have affected the creation of the work.

Memorise these in whichever way works for you and make sure you're ready to call upon them in an exam.

Attempt practice questions/write essay plans. As previously mentioned, quotes are the tools used to write an essay. However, you can't get by with just rattling off every quote that you know – you need to be able to use them appropriately when constructing an argument. We'll talk more about how to write a strong answer in the next section. For now, make sure that you attempt some practice questions. There's a plethora of essay questions available in exams from previous years, so get hold of these and make use of them. If possible, write every essay under exam conditions: no notes, handwritten, in a single sitting and within the time limit. This will test your knowledge as well as your ability to construct a response under pressure.

If writing loads of essays gets boring or tiring, there are other ways you can make use of practice questions when revising. For example, rather than writing the whole answer, you could just write a plan, showing the skeletal structure of an essay. Write out the flow of your essay in brief notes, including:

- What each of your main points/arguments are;

- The quotes and other ideas from the text (e.g. form and structure) that you'd use to support the above point;

- How you'd transition between main points.

Planning essays is useful for several reasons. Firstly, you'll get an idea of how to make an argument flow. Written plans are great if you're a visual learner because you can memorise the page itself. In particular, pay attention to how you move between points – this is what makes an essay look even more sophisticated.

Secondly, getting some good planning practice in is good since you'll need to plan your answer in the exam. By learning to read and dissect a question quickly, as well as making a relevant plan, you'll be better equipped to deal with it during the actual exam.

Finally, planning essays is less intense than writing them, and it's easier to have a teacher or classmate check it for you than a full piece of work. If you do write any essay plans in preparation for your exams, ask your teacher if they'd be happy to read it, and if they could give some brief advice to help you improve.

Make sure you do a combination of planning answers and writing full essays. You gain vital skills from doing both, so it's definitely worth putting in the time to do them!

In the Exam…

In this section, we'll cover the essential skills and tips you'll need in order to write a superb answer, securing you those high marks.

Make it interesting. The examiner marking your paper will likely be reading and assessing tens of other people's exams. By the time they get round to yours, they'll probably be bored of seeing the same quotes and the same arguments being made over and over again. Of course, the examiner will try to be as objective as possible, but nevertheless you should try and make your exam interesting by looking at things from a slightly different angle. You don't need to go over the top in being different – focus on your essays being well-written, first – but an interesting essay will catch the examiner's eye, and might net you some extra marks.

Support your claims. This is the key to doing well in an English Literature exam. You need to construct an argument in which your claims are supported by the text. So, if you argue that the key theme of Wilfrid Owen's *Dulce Et Decorum Est* is the futility of life, you need to be able to demonstrate it with examples in the text. Ideally, you want to follow a structure which allows you to consistently make claims to support your argument. We recommend using a model similar to "Point, Evidence, Explain", but with some adjustments to account for the higher level of writing required at A-Level:

• **Point.** Make your claim – "Owen's *Dulce Et Decorum Est* demonstrates how expendable soldiers are treated."

- **Evidence.** "Old beggars under sacks…" "Many had lost their boots…"

- **Explain.** Explain how the evidence supports your claim – "The state of these soldiers shows that they clearly are no longer fit for combat, yet they are forced to trudge on."

- **Link.** Here, you need to link your entire claim back to the question – "For this reason, it is clear that Owen is attempting to show how fragile human beings are and how they are misused regardless."

All of these steps are important, but linking your argument back to the question at the end of every paragraph is vital. It will help you stay on track with the question and prevent you from slowly spiralling into irrelevance.

Stay relevant. One of the things that's marked highly by A-Level English examiners is relevance, and a commitment to staying relevant throughout your answer. It's too easy to write everything you know that vaguely relates to a topic, but more experienced and eloquent candidates will focus on the strictly relevant details, and still be able to construct a strong response from them. When you plan your answer, take care to read the question carefully and figure out exactly what it's asking. From there, you can write an answer which is concise.

Be confident. Finally, the way to score the highest marks in A-Level English is to do all of the above, but also be confident in your answer. Use assertive and informed language to make confident claims. Don't skirt around topics, get into them!

Sciences

In this section, we'll be covering all three of the 'classical' sciences – biology, chemistry, and physics. While there are differences between the three subjects, we'll be looking at revision and exam tips to help you prepare for any of them.

Sciences at A-Level are straightforward in concept, even if the content is quite difficult. You'll have anywhere between 8 and 10 general modules, each with sub-topics that you'll need to learn. A-Level sciences are also entirely exam-based, which means that you don't need to worry about coursework. Different sciences and different exam boards may vary in the number of exams to be taken.

A-Level science exams are similar across AS and A2, with the only major difference being the actual content and the difficulty. As you might imagine, AS is designed to be less challenging than A2, and the material that you need to study is different. However, you should remember that a lot of A-Level science is cumulative – earlier knowledge informs your understanding of later topics. This means you should give equal attention to each topic, so that you aren't left behind in your studies.

Tips for Science Revision

As previously mentioned, you will need to learn a lot of facts for A-Level sciences. You'll need to learn multiple different concepts depending on the subject or subjects that you're taking. Take a look at our tips for acing A-Level science:

Learn the material. Learning material for the sciences is fairly straightforward, since it mostly boils down to right or wrong answers. Depending on what type of learner you are, there's a range of revision methods that work well for science at A-Level.

If you're a kinaesthetic learner, flashcards can be a great way for matching the names of concepts to their definitions. Write down the name of the concept on one side of the card, then its definition on the reverse. Use this to remind yourself of key ideas that you'll need to draw upon in the exam. Bear in mind that A-Level requires more than just being able to recall key concepts and describe them – you'll probably need to apply them to specific problems and scenarios.

Brush up on your maths. As previously mentioned, you will need to do some mathematical problem solving in your science papers. Calculators are permitted, so you don't need to worry about working on your mental arithmetic, but you will need to remember one or two formulas in order to solve some of the questions. Depending on the subject, year, and exam board, some formulas may be written for you in the opening pages of the exam paper. Have a look at some papers from previous years and see what they give you, then focus on the formulas that you have to remember. There are mnemonics and diagrams which can help make the formulas easier to digest.

Attempt practice papers. As always, practice papers are the best way to get an idea of where you're comfortably scoring marks, and where you need to improve. It's recommended to try and take a paper in one sitting, under timed exam conditions. However, individual questions can be taken from past papers and attempted separately in order to test your knowledge on a specific topic.

For the sciences, the mark scheme is straightforward because the answers are either right or wrong, with little room for ambiguity. This means that you can mark your own paper once you've finished it, or have a friend or family member mark it for you.

In the Exam…

Once the exam starts, write down any of the formulas or key concepts that you know will come up, either on a blank piece of paper or somewhere on your answer booklet (not in an answer box, and remember draw a line through it so the examiner doesn't mark it). This means that you can quickly refer to these notes rather than worrying about remembering them constantly.

Generally, Science exams are split into topics. This means that questions of a similar topic will be grouped together. The questions in a section tend to get more demanding as they progress, and then the difficulty 'curve' of questions will reset once the next section begins. So, you can (and should) start with whichever section you are most comfortable with, complete it, then move onto tougher areas.

Unlike GCSE Science, which consists of lots of short, single-mark questions, A-Level science is a bit more complex. You aren't necessarily going to be asked to give the name of a concept, but you need to know what it is when writing your answer. Make sure to use accurate terminology wherever appropriate so you can show the examiner that you know the material. Sometimes, candidates blank on the exact name of something and try and explain it in vague terms. This might net you some marks in extreme circumstances, but you should try to be as concise as possible. Waffling is painfully obvious to the examiner.

You'll likely have to interpret graphs and data in the exam, so make sure that you're prepared for that. As always, the best way to prepare for these questions is to study some past papers, but make sure to check your working carefully in the actual exam. Make sure you fully read the materials before answering the questions.

Languages

From French to Japanese, there are plenty of languages available for study at A-Level. While all of these languages are very different in terms of grammar, vocabulary and even alphabet, A-Level exam boards tend to approach them in similar ways. In this section, we'll be focusing on the current model used for modern foreign languages, which consists of four main areas: speaking, listening, reading, and writing.

Like GCSE, A-Level language requires that you learn grammar rules and vocabulary, but expects you to take everything a step further. Everything you'll need to learn is more complex – you'll have to apply more sophisticated grammar and vocabulary in your exams –

but the tactics you used at GCSE level in order to revise are still mostly relevant. All that's changed is the content, rather than the structure, of the course.

Before continuing, let's take a look at the four areas of a Language A-Level and what they assess:

- **Reading.** This essentially tests your comprehension skills – your ability to use vocabulary and grammar to understand a text and then answer questions on it. Questions can be asked in either language (English or the language you're studying), and the language you need to answer in will be specified.

- **Listening.** This tests your ability to understand the language you're studying when it's being spoken. You'll be provided with some headphones and sound files to listen to in order to answer the questions. This means you can listen to the files as many times as you need to in order to answer the questions.

- **Writing.** In this part of the course, you'll need to write an extended piece of work about a topic. The topics usually involve the culture, history, or politics of the country that the language you've studied is from. For example, if you're studying Spanish, your topic might be the Spanish Civil War.

- **Speaking.** This is slightly different to the other assessment areas above since it doesn't take place in a formal, written exam. Instead, you'll be asked to take part in a speaking exercise, usually with a languages teacher at your school. You'll be given a topic and some time to formulate an argument or series of discussion points. Then, you'll need to give a form of presentation, which is generally followed up by debate with the teacher. This tests your ability to read, write, listen *and* speak in the language that you're studying. Speaking assessments usually take place a few weeks before the rest of your exams, and are generally worth between 25% and 30% of your AS level or A2 level.

Finally, current Languages exams tend to contain a dedicated grammar section, where you'll be asked to complete a grammar task, such as conjugating verbs or making gender agreements. For this reason, it's important that you know your grammar.

At A-Level, the same kind of exams are sat in both years. The specifics may differ, but you'll be expected to cover all of the above areas at AS level as well as A2 level. Of course, it'll be more demanding at A2.

Tips for Languages Revision

So, we've made it clear that Languages exams test you in a broad range of ways. You'll need to be able to speak, listen, read and write in the language that you're studying, which is no easy feat. Since these four areas of study are so different from one another, we're going to split them up for this section and discuss them individually. However, you may find that revision tips in some sections apply to others.

Reading

Practice your reading. This section essentially involves comprehension. So, it follows that you'll need to be able to read the language that you're studying in order to understand the text, as well as answer in the language as well. This means you need to be able to read the language well. Take some time to read from a wide range of sources in the language that you're studying so that you get used to the way words are used, as well as how to understand the tone of a text. This is particularly helpful if you find things to read which share the topics that your exam will cover. Online resources are great for this since foreign-language news articles can often be accessed easily and for free. You might learn some interesting things about the countries which speak the language, too!

One of the best ways to improve your understanding is to extend your vocabulary, so you're less likely to come across words that you don't understand. Depending on your course, your exam board may release a full vocabulary list, containing all of the words you need to know the meaning of in order to secure a good grade in the assessment. If this is made available to you, make full use of it to construct flashcards, write notes, or record yourself speaking the word in English as well as the language you've studied. Even if an official vocabulary list isn't provided by the exam board, textbooks, workbooks and online resources are available which can be used as a checklist to make sure you know every word necessary.

Don't forget about grammar. Grammar is tested constantly in Languages A-Levels, including reading. Grammar is important because it means you can make sense of sentences in greater detail. It also prevents you from being caught out by questions that specifically refer to different tenses. You should take the time to learn grammar for all of your topics, but make sure to apply it when doing reading as well!

Listening

Spend time listening to the language you're studying. This may seem obvious, but many students don't know where to start when it comes to finding material to listen to. Listening to music in the language that you're studying can be helpful, as you'll become accustomed with the speed and tone of the language, as well as be introduced to a considerable vocabulary – all in easily digestible songs. Films and television are also a safe bet, particularly when they were written and filmed in the language (rather than dubbed in it). You should watch these with English subtitles if it helps – it will give you an insight into how the language is spoken. It doesn't replace revision, but it acts as a great supplement to your studies and can be used as a break from long periods of note-taking.

Learn your vocabulary. A strong vocabulary is incredibly valuable for both listening and reading exams, since you'll need to figure out what words are written or being spoken. 'Vocab lists' are a great way of memorising the words you'll need to know. During your course, you'll be introduced to words associated with certain topics, such as culture, politics, and history. Words revolving around these areas will be likely to show up in your exam, so you should take the time to learn those subjects. Vocab lists will likely be available in your textbooks, as well as appearing in online resources. You can use them by looking at the word, covering up its meaning in English, then writing down what you think it means. Once you can do that easily, do it the other way around – look at the word in English, then write it in the language that you're studying. If possible, use online resources to listen to how the words sound as well. Audio vocabulary lists can be used by listening to a word, then writing down the English translation.

Don't forget about tenses. There are lots of different tenses and verb forms in French and Spanish, and they are vital for getting marks in almost every assessment in languages. Tenses are important in listening tests because you might be asked "true or false" questions that focus on your knowledge of them. For example, the exercise might say "Mark plays football in his spare time" (in the foreign language). You can then be asked the question:

"Mark used to play football regularly." True or False?

If you didn't know your tenses, a question like this could completely catch you out, since the statement in the question says that Mark *used* to play football, which is a different tense to "Mark plays football", the phrase in the listening exercise. Questions like this can show up in the listening exercise, so it's important you take the time to learn them. Online quizzes and games can test your ability to spot which tenses are appropriate for a sentence, and in turn this will help you recognise the tenses as they show up in the exam.

Writing

For the writing exam, you will need to be able to communicate ideas in a written format. This means you'll need to utilise a number of different skills, and have quite a vast pool of knowledge at the ready. All of the above sections on grammar and vocabulary apply here.

Get hold of some practice papers. Past papers and sample questions are going to be useful for several reasons. Firstly, you can use them to practice writing responses to the questions. If possible, give them to your teacher to mark.

The other reason why practice papers are so useful for this exam is that there's a range of different types of question, and you need to prepare yourself for them. There are open-ended writing tasks, closed writing tasks and translation exercises, amongst other activities in the writing exam. With such a large variety, you need to familiarise yourself with what these types of question look like, and what's expected of you.

Speaking

Preparing for the speaking assessment is very different to studying for other exams. Unlike almost every other exam you'll take at A-Level, you aren't assessed on written work in the speaking assessment, but rather your ability to communicate ideas clearly by speaking in a foreign language.

Speaking tests take place earlier than other exams.

You'll probably sit your speaking assessment a few weeks earlier than you sit the rest of your exams. This can be a problem for people who don't take this into account, but if you know what you're doing, you can benefit from having this come earlier. Make sure your revision for the speaking test takes place earlier in the revision period, so you have as much time to study for it as possible.

Listen to how people speak. By no means are you expected to have a perfect accent, but knowing how words are pronounced is necessary for making sure you can communicate effectively during the speaking test. Listening to music and finding audio examples of conversation in the language online will give you an idea of what tone people use when speaking, and how the words are pronounced.

Prepare for everything. You won't know the exact topic of your listening assessment, so unfortunately you can't revise for precisely what you're going up against. Instead, you need to get a list of possible topics and prepare for all of them. This might sound time-consuming, but it's better to cover as many bases as possible to prevent coming across a topic that you haven't prepared for.

Be appropriate. The speaking test focuses on appropriate use of vocabulary and grammar, so make sure you stick to the point and don't go overboard. Waffle or filling space to make your answers and conversation seem more sophisticated than they are won't work – try to be direct as possible with your answers.

Be ready to show some flair. This seems to contradict

the last point, but it's important that you're ready to show off your abilities in the assessment. After all, the point of the speaking assessment is to test your ability to speak the language. This means that you want to show that you have access to a wide vocabulary, and that you're able to use grammatical conventions effectively. You don't want to go overboard with it, but make sure that you're able to show all of the skills that they're looking for. Try and find a balance between being functional and showing your skills.

Practice the scenario. Depending on your specification, the scenario your speaking exam takes place in could differ. In some cases, it just involves a discussion, but others may find that they need to give a presentation on a topic and then field questions from their teacher. Make sure you know what you're getting into, and practice the whole assessment from start to finish.

Practice with a friend. The speaking assessment is unique because, unlike exams, it requires two people to be carried out. This means that practising the exercise can be difficult when you're on your own. So, try and enlist the help of a classmate who's also studying the same language. Find some practice questions or topics, then take turns being the assessor whilst the other is the exam candidate. If possible, try and get hold of a mark scheme so that you know what to look out for when you're assessing the other person. This means you can give them advice once they've finished.

In the Exam…

Languages exams are quite varied in terms of content

and structure, and you're going to be tested on different things in each. There are, however, a few tips that apply to all of them:

Complete the exam in any order that you like. While each section covers a different topic, you can start anywhere. Try and start with the sections and questions that you find easiest, then work your way up.

Finish the writing section last. If you find this section easiest, ignore this tip. Otherwise, consider the following. Firstly, the writing section is usually a more open-ended task, so it's harder to gauge how long to spend on it. If you do the writing task first, you run the risk of spending too much time on it and then not having enough time to finish the other sections. If you leave the writing task to last, then you know you can dedicate the rest of the exam to it. Secondly, you might pick up some words in the reading and listening sections which jog your memory, giving you more to write about. For this reason, it's worth leaving the writing task to the end.

Write down key vocabulary straight away. As soon as the exam starts, write down anything you think you'll need to know on your answer booklet (not in an answer box) so that you don't need to keep it stored in your mind. If you've got something to refer to when writing your answers, you'll likely feel less stressed.

History

A-Level History is incredibly different to its GCSE counterpart. At GCSE, you were expected to remember key facts, dates and names, then be able to recall them in the exam. While a small amount of interpretation and critical analysis may have been going on in the more demanding questions, you were mostly being tested on how well you knew the material, as opposed to how well you could discuss it.

At A-Level, this changes entirely. Instead of being tested on sheer knowledge, you now need to show a deeper understanding of events, and be able to interpret history in order to answer questions in a critical manner. In this sense, A-Level History isn't too different to A-Level English. You need to make claims in relation to the question and then support them with evidence such as statistics, quotes, or other facts. After that, you need to demonstrate how this supports your claim by explaining your evidence.

What you study in A-Level History is determined by a number of different factors. Firstly, exam boards choose a few general areas of study, ranging from Germany 1890-1945 to the History of Medicine. Some of these will be available for examination, whilst others will be coursework modules.

Generally speaking, A-Level History students will complete one piece of coursework, usually at A2. This is a research task, which involves candidates reading about a topic, and answering either one or two extended questions. Generally, this is a slightly more controlled piece of coursework, so you might not be able to take it home with you and complete it there. You'll be given plenty of time to conduct your research, so make sure you have a library card at the ready.

The coursework will also test your ability to structure a piece of work in a way that would be accepted by university academics. You'll have to find sources and cite them effectively in your work in order to support your answer. This is something you'll have to do in the exam, but here you'll need to add footnotes and a bibliography to make your coursework look the part.

Tips for History Revision

Get your facts straight. Knowing facts is vitally important for doing well at History A-Level. Just being able to recall events isn't enough to secure the higher marks (more on this later), but knowledge of events is vital for being able to critically analyse historical figures and events. Go through your materials and take note of key facts and statistics that you can use in an argument.

There's a vast amount of knowledge necessary in order to do well in A-Level History. Since you don't know what topics will appear in the exam, you're expected to know about basically everything. This seems harsh, but you'll be rewarded well if you can manage it. It's important that you contextualise every piece of information that you study. Think about the following when revising facts and statistics:

- How does this relate to the current topic?

- Which historical figures/groups are directly affected by these facts?

- How big a role did these facts play in changing the course of history?

...se these facts effectively in an answer?

...ou want to revise these facts is entirely up ...visual learners will do well here because of the si... bulk of work that can be written out as notes, then internalised over time. However, aural learners could make use of talking through all of these facts with a classmate or family member until they feel confident. If you're working with a classmate, you have the bonus of them picking up on things that you've missed, and vice versa.

Learn to interpret facts and link them to a question. Being able to interpret facts and form an argument is the most important skill you'll learn for A-Level History. Not only will learning to do this enforce some good habits for further academia (such as university), but it will also make sure you can get the top marks. As previously mentioned, knowing and being able to list off facts is only a small part of where you get your marks from. What's just as important is how you link them to the question. The way you do this is by structuring an argument.

In order to create an argument, you need to be able to think critically about information you read. A good way to do this is to write a possible exam question down, then write a series of key facts and statistics that you think may relate to the question. Then, you need to fill the gap between the question and these facts. You don't want to be fitting any old facts to the question – try to keep it as relevant as possible. We'll talk more about using essay plans to structure arguments later on.

Another thing to consider is historical interpretation. By

this, we mean researching what historians have written about the events and figures that you've studied. The interpretations that historians have made can be used as a means of supporting your argument in an exam, or they can simply be a means of pointing you in the right direction. Whatever the case, make sure you have a few of these handy to add some variety and flair to your answers.

Read some books. This probably sounds ridiculous, but actually reading some books as a part of History revision can work wonders. Many students will read the textbooks they've been given as well as any other materials given by their teacher, but not nearly as many will get out there and conduct their own research. Reading from a range of sources is valuable for the following reasons:

- It gives you a broader variety of historical inter-pretations to draw from when answering an essay question;

- It does a lot of contextualisation of facts and statistics for you (i.e. they'll explain why certain figures, events and facts are important);

- It provides further information that might not have been made explicit in your textbooks;

- It will go into much greater detail on many issues than the core textbooks.

Generally speaking, core textbooks are designed to be introductory material, and you should treat them as such. Extended reading is vital for A-Level History (particularly

A2) so make sure to get a list of relevant texts from your teacher and read some of them.

Write some essay plans. Essay plans are a great way of revising since they force you to think about how your ideas all fit together. You might have pages upon pages of notes, but if you can't structure them all into an argument then you won't be able to complete the exam properly. To make use of essay plans effectively, do the following:

1. Choose an essay question either from a textbook or a past paper.

2. Underline the key points of the question:

- What is the question asking me to do (e.g. compare, analyse, critically assess)?

- What do I need to write about?

3. Write down your argument as briefly as possible (e.g. "Adolf Hitler's trial was the most influential event during his rise to power").

4. Try to come up with as many main points as possible – these are the reasons why you believe the claim you made in step 3 (e.g. "His public trial meant that his beliefs were broadcast to millions of disillusioned Germans).

5. Provide facts and statistics for each of these points so that you're grounding them in fact.

6. Explain how this relates to the point that you've made.

Do this for every point that you make in your essay.

There's no set amount of points you should make – you are marked on how well you argue your points, not how many you come up with. This means you need to figure out for yourself how many well-realised points you can fit into the time limit. To figure that out, you're going to have to...

Make use of practice papers. Practice papers are useful for History A-Level for the same reasons they're handy for English. Not only do they give you an opportunity to test your knowledge, but they also check whether you're able to apply everything you know to a strong argument. If you can write a well-fleshed out argument, then you know you're ready for the exam. Additionally, practice papers written under timed conditions will help you figure out how long it takes you to answer a question, and how much you can write about. The more of these you do, the better you'll get at timing.

Read the mark scheme. History is somewhat like Maths in that you are dealing with facts, but a bit more like English because you need to discuss them, analyse them and in some cases form arguments. By reading the mark scheme, you get an idea of what types of things examiners are looking for. However, this isn't like GCSE where all you need to do is say the right things and jump through hoops. Instead, A-Level History assesses your ability to form and maintain concise and nuanced arguments. Therefore, the mark schemes might be a bit more nebulous than those of a Maths or Science paper. Regardless, they'll give you an idea of what to do in the exam. They'll also let you know how marks are broken down.

In the Exam…

As previously mentioned, the most important thing to remember about History exams is that you're there to form strong arguments, rather than just recite facts. You'll be asked to demonstrate knowledge from a vast area of History, but not every fact you know will be relevant. Therefore, be sparing with your use of statistics and facts – only use what's strictly relevant to the question.

What's more important is that you make a series of points and argue them effectively. The "Point, Evidence, Explain, Link" model mentioned earlier in this chapter (in the section on English Literature) is relevant here – all you need to do is replace the quotes from the English paper with historical facts. In many ways, you can treat it like any other essay-based exam. Remember to do the following:

• Spend some time planning each answer;

• Make sure to read the question carefully, and make note of key details in it;

• Clearly show what question you're answering so that the examiner knows how to mark your essay;

• Always answer the question.

Geography

A-Level Geography consists of exams and a field assignment. For the exams, you'll be expected to learn about both human and physical geography. Generally speaking, the exams are divided to match these categories. So, you might find that you have to sit two exams at A2: one for human geography, and one for physical geography. The field assignment is usually some kind of field trip combined with coursework – you'll have to complete a project based on what research you do on the field trip. In some cases, this has to be completed under exam conditions.

As a subject, Geography sits somewhere between the sciences and a History paper. You need to know your facts, be able to solve problems, and interpret data. At the same time, you'll be asked to analyse things, and possibly even critically assess concepts. There are plenty of essay questions which will test your ability not only to recall information, but to also use it to evaluate views about physical and human geography.

Tips for Geography Revision

Learn key terms. This is just as important at A-Level as it is at GCSE, but with the added challenge of knowing how different concepts apply to different questions. In other words, you can just read the vocabulary lists and memorise them – you also need to be able to apply them in context. To an extent, you'll need to be able to think on your feet when making use of what you know. So, make sure that you know all of the words that may be used in questions, as well as all of the concepts and terms that you need to remember.

Complete your coursework to the best of your ability. This might sound obvious, but plenty of students neglect their coursework because they think they can just make up the marks in their exam, or the lack of strict time constraints doesn't motivate them to complete their controlled assessments adequately. Think of it this way: the better you perform in your coursework, the more marks you'll have going into the exam. Coursework is an excellent opportunity to bank marks and have them secured. So, if anything does happen to go wrong in the exam – say you're unlucky with the questions given, or you blank on key information – it isn't the end of the world because you'll have already scored some points in the coursework.

In the Exam…

Geography exams require several different skills from you, and these are tested in different ways. You'll be asked to identify correct and incorrect statements in multiple-choice questions, assess claims made in the paper, and demonstrate whether or not you agree with a specific point of view. Make sure you're familiar with all the different kinds of question. Also, keep note of what kinds of question that you're being asked. If it helps, underline the key terms in the question (e.g. 'evaluate', 'assess', 'identify').

Social Sciences

In this section, we're going to discuss Psychology and Sociology, which are the 'social sciences'. While there are significant differences between the two in terms of content, they both exist in a unique space that separates them from both the 'classical' sciences (Chemistry, Physics, Biology) and the humanities (History, Geography). They rely on examining data and doing experiments, but at the same time have enough elbow room for critical analysis and analysis. For this reason, we're going to cover the two together.

At A-Level, these subjects are exam-based, and the content of the exams covers a vast range of topics and question types. Some questions might only expect brief description for a few marks, whilst long essays will be introduced towards the end, usually demanding an assessment of a statement.

This combination of question types means you need to know a number of things. Firstly, you need to know the facts – key theories and hypotheses, as well as how to apply them in both descriptive and evaluative contexts. Unlike a lot of other subjects, you also need to be able to draw upon case studies and key scientific projects and experiments. In many cases, you need to be specific about the names of researchers, their hypothesis, and their methodology. This is particularly the case for Psychology, but is also relevant for Sociology. With this in mind, let's take a look at the best ways to revise for the social sciences.

Tips for Social Sciences Revision

Research and case studies are vital. As previously mentioned, you need to remember the key details from research conducted, as well as more anecdotal case studies. When studying research, try to focus on the following:

- The names of the researcher(s);

- The year that the paper was published;

- The hypothesis of the researchers prior to research;

- How the research was conducted (i.e. what was the experiment?);

- The methodology used to collect and interpret data;

- The implications of the study (i.e. what does the study suggest? Does it support the hypothesis?);

- Ethical concerns (i.e. was the experiment ethical?).

All of these will be important for different questions. For example, a long essay question might ask you to evaluate a claim, and you'll have to refer to relevant studies in order to support your argument. This means you'll need to know the names of the researchers and the year the study was published so that you can cite them as a source. Then, you'll need to know the details of the study, and how you can relate it to the argument that you're making in the question. Other questions might be simpler, instead asking you to recount the elements of the study and then come to some conclusion about it. In either case, you need to spend a considerable amount of time studying cases and research in order to perform well.

Prepare for different kinds of question. The type of questions in social sciences papers can vary from multiple-choice to long essay. The best way to make sure that you're ready for such a wide range of questions is to take a look at practice papers and mark schemes. Remember that different kinds of question will assess different abilities, so read mark schemes and examiners' reports to find out exactly what you need to do in order to score top marks.

In the Exam...

For the social sciences, you need to remember to substantiate all of your claims. While you are often asked to evaluate claims and offer your own thoughts, you must make sure that every claim you make is supported by evidence. For example, you might be asked to evaluate the claim that human beings are more like to co-operate with authority when they can't see the victims of their orders. You might begin by saying that, while Milgram (1963) seems to support this view, the fact that the experiment took place under artificial conditions means that it doesn't necessarily represent the behaviour of people in the real world. You might then use this to argue that we simply don't know either way whether not being able to see the victim increases the likelihood of compliance.

Conclusion

So, now we've taken a look at some of the most popular subjects at A-Level and how to revise effectively for them. We've also discussed exam tactics for each of the subjects, so hopefully you feel more equipped (or at least more assured) to take them on. Before we wrap up this section, it's important to reiterate the following two points.

Firstly, check your exam board website for exact details. In this guide, we've discussed specific subjects in as much detail as we can. However, the specifics will differ depending on exam board and the year you sit the exam. Syllabuses tend to change every few years, so it's important to stay as up to date as possible.

Secondly, make use of all the advice in this chapter. Even if you aren't taking every subject we've discussed, it's worth looking through all of these sections anyway. This is because there's plenty of cross-pollination between subjects, and taking an unconventional approach to your revision might be exactly what you need to be successful.

What Next?

So, now you have all of the facts, tips, and advice from experts on how to pass your A-Levels with A*s. You might be now be thinking about what you want to do next, after you've aced your A-Levels and want to go on to the next stage in your life. In this chapter, we'll take a look at the following:

- How to make use of your A-Levels;

- University and employment;

- How to apply for university;

- Employment ideas.

Making Use of Your A-Levels

Once you're working on your A-Levels, you need to think about what you want to do next. You don't have to apply for university or jobs while you're taking your A-Levels, but it is common practice for those studying at A-Level to also be creating a personal statement and applying to universities. However, you can apply for university later if you'd like to put it off for a year or so.

Whether you're heading to university or going into employment, your A-Levels will be valuable. For university, you'll need A-Levels in order to get yourself a place with essentially zero exceptions. If you're currently studying A-Levels and are waiting for results, universities will give you "conditional offers". This means that, provided you meet the grades they set when you get your results, the university will have saved a space for you.

The grades required will differ based on your circumstances and the standards set by the university, whilst the subjects required will differ depending on what you wish to study. For example, students wishing to study Physics at degree level will be expected to have an A-Level in Physics as well as an A-Level in Maths. From there, A-Levels in Chemistry and Biology would also be preferable, but this will change depending on the university. You probably had a vague idea of what you'd like to study prior to choosing your A-Levels, but from here you need to specialise. Your A-Levels will point you in the right direction.

As for employment, you need to think about how the subjects you've studied demonstrate your skills. For example, high grades in subjects such as History and English Literature demonstrate a critical eye and the ability to structure arguments, which would be invaluable in many industries. So, you need to take time to think about what your A-Levels could be used to do, how they sell you as a candidate, and what roles and careers they suit.

University

University is a great option for students who wish to pursue academics a step further, and maybe get into some kind of career only accessible from possessing a degree. Doctors, lawyers, lecturers, and teachers all require a degree in relevant fields in order for you to become one. So, if any of those fields interest you, make sure that you take the time to read up on them and what they require from you.

Once you've found a career that you like the look of, you need to know how to get into university. Take a look at our rundown of the application process:

- Create a UCAS account to begin your application. If you are currently a student studying A-Levels, your school may have already done this for you;

- Start thinking of things you've done (or can do) that can support your personal statement;

- Study for your A-Levels (using this book!);

- Apply for the universities that you like the look of and you think you can get into;

- Wait for offers to come back (these appear in the first half of the calendar year);

- Make your 'firm' and 'insurance' choices;

- Sit your exams and complete your coursework;

- Confirm your university choices once you get your results in August.

Depending on your school, you'll have classes which will guide you through this process. Make sure that you take these seriously so that you get your application completed in time!

In order to successfully apply for university, you'll need the following:

- Completed A-Levels (or predicted A-Levels if you're still studying) to a grade specified by the universities you apply to;

- A UCAS application which includes your GCSE grades, A-Level (either predicted or actual) grades, a personal statement, and written references from your school.

If you have all of these, you'll be in a position to apply for university. From there, you'll have the opportunity to complete your degree, which will strengthen your career prospects even further!

You'll also need to consider that university is expensive. However, you can apply for a student loan and get the support you need to live at university as well as pay for your tuition. Get the facts about student loans, but don't let yourself be put off an incredible opportunity just because you're afraid of paying it off.

Employment

While going to university is an excellent experience that many enjoy, this isn't the only path to a successful career and a happy life. In fact, heading straight into work is preferable for people who aren't fussed about university life, and want to get into the workplace as soon as possible. Here are some pros and cons of heading straight into work after finishing A-Levels:

Pros	Cons
Gets you onto the career ladder quicker	You miss out on great university experiences (you can always go later, though!)

Exposes you to life and work experiences that you wouldn't get at university	Some careers require a degree that you can only get from university
Saves you money on student loans	University can give you other hobbies and skills which help your career advancement
Allows you to take other routes such as apprenticeships	

As you can see, there are good reasons to skip university if you don't think it's for you. There are pros and cons to attending university as well as heading straight into employment. Take some time to consider which route is best for you.

Employment – What Should I Do?

When leaving A-Levels, it can be hard to figure out where to start with your career. Some people know exactly where to begin, whilst others have no idea what they want to go into. We can't tell you exactly what career is right for you, but we can point you in the right direction. Visit www.how2become.com for a list of careers and professions in the public and private sectors, as well as guides and testing materials for each of them.

Conclusion

So, you now know all the tips we can give you for acing your A-Levels. You've learnt what A-Levels are, how they're marked and graded, and why they matter. You've also been introduced to several revision techniques, and hopefully had the opportunity to find out what type of learner you are. In addition, you've been given the rundown on exams and coursework, and you know how to combat stress. Finally, we've provided some subject-specific advice so that you can focus your studies and get the best marks possible.

One thing to take away from this book is that A-Levels aren't the most important thing in the world. They might feel like that while you're studying for them, with what feels like a mountain to overcome, but once they're over and you get your results, you should feel satisfied (and proud) of what you've accomplished. Make use of the tips we've provided in this book, try your best, and go away from your A-Levels knowing that you've done something impressive and commendable.

A Few Final Words...

You have reached the end of your guide to passing your A-Levels with A*s. If you have read the information in this book and made use of the tips provided, you should be on your way to passing your A-Levels comfortably and making yourself proud. Hopefully, you will feel far more confident in what you know as well as what you need to improve.

For any test, it is helpful to consider the following in mind...

The Three 'P's

1. Preparation. Preparation is key to passing any test; you won't be doing yourself any favours by not taking the time to prepare. Many fail their tests because they did not know what to expect or did not know what their own weaknesses were. Take the time to re-read any areas you may have struggled with. By doing this, you will become familiar with how you will perform on the day of the test.

2. Perseverance. If you set your sights on a goal and stick to it, you are more likely to succeed. Obstacles and setbacks are common when trying to achieve something great, and you shouldn't shy away from them. Instead, face the tougher parts of the test, even if you feel defeated. If you need to, take a break from your work to relax and then return with renewed vigour. If you fail the test, take the time to consider why you failed, gather your strength and try again.

3. Performance. How well you perform will be the result of your preparation and perseverance. Remember to relax when taking the test and try not to panic. Believe in your own abilities, practice as much as you can, and motivate yourself constantly. Nothing is gained without hard work and determination, and this applies to how you perform on the day of the test.

Good luck with your A-Levels. We wish you the best of luck in all of your future endeavours!

Useful
Resources

	Monday	Tuesday	Wednesday	Thursday	Friday	Saturday	Sunday
09:00am - 10:00am							
10:00am - 11:00am							
11:00am - 12:00pm							
12:00pm - 01:00pm							
01:00pm - 02:00pm							

	Monday	Tuesday	Wednesday	Thursday	Friday	Saturday	Sunday
02:00pm - 03:00pm							
03:00pm - 04:00pm							
04:00pm - 05:00pm							
05:00pm - 06:00pm							
06:00pm - 07:00pm							

	Monday	Tuesday	Wednesday	Thursday	Friday	Saturday	Sunday
09:00am - 10:00am							
10:00am - 11:00am							
11:00am - 12:00pm							
12:00pm - 01:00pm							
01:00pm - 02:00pm							

	Monday	Tuesday	Wednesday	Thursday	Friday	Saturday	Sunday
02:00pm - 03:00pm							
03:00pm - 04:00pm							
04:00pm - 05:00pm							
05:00pm - 06:00pm							
06:00pm - 07:00pm							

	Monday	Tuesday	Wednesday	Thursday	Friday	Saturday	Sunday
09:00am - 10:00am							
10:00am - 11:00am							
11:00am - 12:00pm							
12:00pm - 01:00pm							
01:00pm - 02:00pm							

	Monday	Tuesday	Wednesday	Thursday	Friday	Saturday	Sunday
02:00pm - 03:00pm							
03:00pm - 04:00pm							
04:00pm - 05:00pm							
05:00pm - 06:00pm							
06:00pm - 07:00pm							

WANT TO IMPROVE YOUR MEMORY AND LEARN EVEN MORE REVISION TRICKS?

CHECK OUT OUR OTHER REVISION GUIDES:

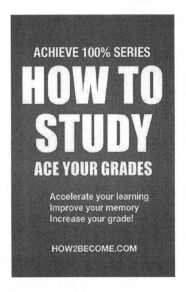

FOR MORE INFORMATION ON OUR REVISION GUIDES, PLEASE CHECK OUT THE FOLLOWING:

WWW.HOW2BECOME.COM

Get Access To

FREE

Psychometric

Tests

www.MyEducationalTests.co.uk